Stress
and the Woman Manager

Stress
and the Woman Manager

MARILYN DAVIDSON
and
CARY COOPER

St. Martin's Press · New York

ISBN 0-312-76610-6

Library of Congress Cataloging in Publication Data

Davidson, Marilyn.
  Stress and the woman manager.

  Bibliography: p. 217
  Includes index.
  1. Job stress—Great Britain.   2. Women
executives—Great Britain.   3. Women middle
managers—Great Britain.   I. Cooper, Cary L.
II. Title.
HF5548.85.D38 1983   658.4′09′088042   83-9666

ISBN 0-321-76610-6

This book is dedicated to David Nicholls, who spent the last few months of his life giving us valuable computing assistance and endless support and encouragement.

Contents

Preface and acknowledgements

Research on the problems faced by women in management has, until now, concentrated on women in senior positions, that is, those who have already overcome any barriers to success. We felt that it was time for in-depth research that would identify the specific problems experienced by women at *all* levels of management, examine the stress that is so often the outcome of women's entry into this male-dominated world, and compare women's experiences in management with those of their male counterparts.

This study was undertaken to provide such information. It is based on a large-scale survey we carried out for the British Government's Manpower Services Commission, on a large sample of female managers across a variety of companies and industries in the UK. We have aimed to highlight the problems of both women and men managers which emerged from our research and link our findings specifically to ways of dealing with the problems. The material that emerges is of importance to women and men managers, their employers, management trainees and trainers, management students and all those interested in management and/or occupational stress.

We are indebted to the Manpower Services Commission Training Division for financing this research project. We would also like to thank the many women and men managers who gave their time and enthusiasm by participating in this study, Dr Rachel Davies Cooper for her excellent graphic design work and our secretary Kathryn Wilkinson for her care and patience.

Marilyn Davidson
Cary Cooper

CHAPTER 1

The position of women in management

Hilary is 28 years of age, and is one of the 696 women managers who answered our survey questionnaires aimed at isolating the problems faced by female managers compared with their male counterparts. Below are the additional comments she wrote, describing her own personal experiences:

I am the Officer in Charge of a small, but busy city centre Job centre. I have been in the Civil Service since 1973, since 1976 as an Executive Officer. I was deputy Officer in Charge at my present office since 1977. Taking up full command in July 1981, I have charge of seven staff, of which only two are men. (This reflects the usual female:male ratio in the Civil Service, where the lower clerical grades are predominantly female.) At present I am blessed with a group of staff who are uniformly bright and co-operative. This enables me to get by with a 'low-profile' as a manager, so that I only need to emerge as a 'leader' when the situation requires me to make decisions. I believe that a man in this position would perhaps feel he had to exert his authority more and be 'seen' to manage. I believe that being in the management role panders to the male ego. The female doesn't believe in wasting energy in striking attitudes about her job as a manager. Women regard management as a job to be done while men see it as something that enhances their status. I find that my female colleagues are less concerned with status than with doing an efficient job. They feel that as women they have to be so much better than men in a similar role in order to prove their capabilities to higher management which, in the Civil Service, is predominantly male.

In the past five years all my immediate managers have been male. Their styles have demonstrated a wide variety of attitudes. There was an elderly gentleman, near retirement, who was one of the 'Old School'. I was treated with a paternal kindness by him which was rather more bearable than being made to feel like a silly female irritant by the next, aggressive, go-getting manager I had. One manager known for his chauvinism, who frequently pestered female staff, treated me reasonably, mainly because I did a good job for him and had an intellectual approach to the job which probably alarmed him so that he kept his distance. My present manager is a model to all those who seek to deal with female staff. He never makes the sexist jokes that one has heard so often before; he treats me as his equal in every respect and consults me as one of his management team rather than as a mere woman. My views are listened to and valued, and this is a rare treat. Unfortunately this situation does not extend to my senior manager who seems ill at ease when he is with his women managers. My constant problem is lack of staff resources, yet if I mention this to him he responds as though I were a nagging wife. It's the 'Oh Hilary, not that again' approach, as though he were chiding his wife for bringing up the price of the children's shoes again. I rather doubt if his male managers get this approach. I have to attend management meetings at which I am frequently the only female. At first it was rather like entering an exclusive Men's Club. I was tolerated but not taken seriously. When the tea arrived I was obviously expected to get up and hand the cups round, this I have steadfastly refused to do! During the course of these meetings I am able to observe how many vacillating, boorish and silly men have wormed their way to the top. Unfortunately this observation has not yet given me sufficient confidence to present myself at their meetings in a really forceful way, even though I know that I am the intellectual superior of most of those present.

Of course the main difference between male and female managers is that for most women their working day does not end at 5.00 pm. Even in these supposedly enlightened times, it is the rare man who contributes significantly to the running of the home. How many men spend their lunch times queueing in the supermarket or dashing round to collect the dry-cleaning? Running even a two-person household takes more time and energy than is generally realized and it is not uncommon for me to spend four or five hours a day on matters connected with a home. The only fringe benefit of this kind of life is that you do get used to organizing your time and energy with a military precision that makes the average MD seem, by comparison, a ditherer. For women with young families the demands on their energy and patience must be enormous and we should hardly be surprised if they do complain of fatigue and feel torn between the demands of home and work. Personally, I always try to encourage the suitably able female members of my staff to look at their job in terms of a career. I encourage and advise them to find that quite often they have a poor image of themselves in relation to their work and lack the confidence to put themselves forward as candidates for promotion. Where their husbands are engaged in manual work, it is common to find that they regard their wives as sort of 'non-workers' simply because they sit at a desk all day rather than being engaged in some sort of 'productive' work.

The general feeling is then that to succeed in management one has to be positively better than one's male counterpart. The road to success is not easy. Some women adopt a simpering and fawning attitude to their superiors in an effort to please. The woman who is independent and wants to be treated on equal terms is still regarded as something of an oddity.

Having read through what I've just written, I wonder if I'm perhaps taking an over-sensitive line, but I have to attend a managers' meeting tomorrow and I know I shall encounter there all the attitudes I have described that make it so difficult to be a woman manager.

It is because of increasing cases like Hilary's that the problems of women in management are drawing national and international attention. In most Western countries, the role of women in society is radically changing. According to the US Labour Department, the traditional 'typical American family' with a homemaker wife, two children and a working husband, now makes up only 7 per cent of the nation's families. Table 1.1 shows that in the UK the trend is the same and only 5 per cent of all households are made up of working husband, economically inactive wife and two dependent children (the *General Household Survey*, 1980).

In addition, 25 years ago, only a quarter of the women who were working were married, by 1980, three-fifths of married women under 60 years of age went out to work. Moreover, women who leave work before and during the early years of motherhood, are re-entering the labour force at a higher rate in Great Britain than in any other country in Western Europe (Lockwood, 1981). Figures published in the Office of Population and Census Studies *General Household Survey* show that the number of working mothers has in

TABLE 1.1   ECONOMIC ACTIVITY OF WOMEN IN BRITAIN IN 1980

Women aged 16–59, by marital status	Percentage of women who		
	work full-time	work part-time	are economically active
Single	61	4	74
Widowed, divorced or separated	38	24	68
All non-married	54	10	72
Married	26	33	62
All women	34	26	65

Working mothers aged 16–59, by age of youngest child	Percentage of women		
	working full-time	working part-time	All work
0–4 years	7	23	30
5–9 years	14	47	62
10 years and over	29	41	71
All with dependent children	17	36	54
No dependent children	50	17	68
All women	34	26	61

Source: General Household Survey preliminary results for 1980 (Monitor GHS 81/1)

fact increased from 45 per cent of all women with children, to 51 per cent during the period 1973–80.

Unfortunately, there is little evidence to suggest that the implementation of the Sex Discrimination Act and Equal Pay Act, which came into force in 1975 has succeeded in alleviating job segregation and unequal pay. Occupational segregation of the sexes: the arbitrary division between 'men's jobs' and 'women's jobs' still persists with nearly two-thirds of employed women being concentrated in occupations including cleaners, teachers, textile operators, shop assistants and clerical service workers. This type of segregation is not the case for men (Robarts, Coote and Ball, 1981). Among professional groups, 22 per cent of doctors are women, 4 per cent of architects, 7 per cent of barristers, 14 per cent of dentists and 0.5 per cent of engineers (Robarts, et al. 1981). Furthermore, table 1.2 shows that in 1981 a woman working full-time earns only 74.8 per cent of what a

TABLE 1.2 EARNINGS

Average gross hourly earnings, excluding overtime, of full-time employees aged 18 and over, whose pay was not affected by absence: women's as a percentage of men's

1970	63.1	1979	73.0
1975	72.1	1981	74.8
1977	75.7		

Average gross weekly earnings, full-time men aged 21 and over, full-time women aged 18 and over whose pay was not affected by absence (April 1981)

	Men	Women	Women's pay as a percentage of men's
Manual	£121.9	£74.6	61.2
Non-manual	£163.1	£86.7	59.3
ALL	£140.6	£91.4	65.0

Source: Gazette, Oct. 1981 (see Social Trends, 1981)

man earns per hour and only 65 per cent of what a man earns per week.

With the recession and unemployment, more women are losing their jobs than men (*Social Trends, 1981*). However, on a brighter note, with more women now working than ever before, there is also a substantial increase in the number of women entering many of the formerly male dominated jobs, including the field of management. According to a review of *Social Trends* by *New Society* (1981): 'The representative working woman may now be a middle-aged wife working part-time at a job with very limited career prospects, but more recent generations of women appear to be moving into better occupations and improving their economic position relative to men' (*New Society*, p. 310). Table 1.3 shows comparative figures for the USA and some European countries and in the majority of these countries women constitute between 15 and 25 per cent of managers and administrators.

In the USA, with the strongest legislation affecting the employment of women, 23.6 per cent of managers and administrators are women, followed by the UK with 18.8 per

TABLE 1.3   WOMEN AS A PERCENTAGE OF ADMINISTRATIVE AND
            MANAGERIAL WORKERS IN SELECTED COUNTRIES

Country	Year	Total (including independent and family workers)	Salaried and wage-earning workers
France	1975		16.3
German Federal Republic	1978	15.6	16.7
Norway	1978	14.6	14.2
Spain	1978	1.5	2.4
Sweden	1975	11.4	11.2
UK*	1979	16.3	18.8
USA	1978	23.5	23.6

Sources: ILO Yearbook of Labour Statistics, Geneva 1979
* EC Labour Force Survey 1979
Note: The occupational classifications for UK are not identical with those for other countries. See forthcoming report by the DE on the EC Labour Force Survey to be published by HMSO.

cent. Even so, in the UK, the occupations in which women are most likely to be managers are traditionally female occupations such as retailing, catering and personnel. As well, in the UK, the highest percentage of women managers are located in the South East including Greater London, with the lowest percentage found in Northern Ireland. (See table 1.4.)

At senior levels of management there are fewer women and only 8.3 per cent of general management jobs are held by women (Training Services Division, Manpower Services Commission, 1981). In this respect, once again the American situation is somewhat better. For example, in 1982, 36 per cent of corporate boards in the USA now have women directors, as opposed to 11 per cent in 1973 (Brown, 1982). However, in Britain, of the top 100 UK companies, only two had women directors in 1979 (McRae, 1980).

Despite this, the UK University Statistical Record shows that from the early to late 1970s, there was a 33 per cent increase in women graduates entering industrial employment; the number of women in finance and accounting rose from 14 to 23 per cent in that period; in legal work from 25

TABLE 1.4   FEMALE MANAGERS AS A PERCENTAGE OF
TOTAL MANAGERS (OCCUPATION CATEGORY GROUP 6)
VIA REGION IN THE UK, 1977

Region	Women managers as percentage of all managers
North	5.5
Yorkshire and Humberside	8.8
North West	14.0
East Midlands	7.6
West Midlands	8.7
East Anglia	3.8
South East including SE Greater London	16.1 ⎫
Greater London	12.7 ⎬ 28.8
South West	8.1 ⎭
Wales	6.1
Scotland	8.6
Northern Ireland	2.6

Source: EEC Labour Force Survey, 1977.

to 32 per cent; in personnel management from 51 to 62 per
cent; and in marketing, selling and buying from 28 to 36 per
cent. This trend has been reinforced by the increasing
number of women taking university courses in management.
With regard to the main universities running undergraduate
courses in management in the UK, the number rose from
187 in 1973, to 770 in 1977; as a proportion of the total
management students, the percentage increased from 12 to
27 per cent; and in the three largest university management
departments, the increase was from roughly 10 to 35 per cent
in that same period (Cooper and Lewis, 1979). In 1981 over
40 per cent of the total management students in the largest
university management department were female. Similar
upward trends are taking place in the US with 28 per cent
of the students in the top American Business Schools being
women. Also, about 15 per cent of today's management
trainees in the US are women, compared with only 1 per
cent in the mid-1960s (Brown, 1982).

A recent British survey of 770 female management
students found that 43 per cent believed that there was a

distinct disadvantage in being a woman and desiring a career in management (Cooper and Lewis, 1979). It is of interest to note that a comparative study of female and male business graduates from the Manchester Business School found that most of the women did not reach the same level of achievement in their careers as their male counterparts. In addition, the women's salaries after graduation were, on average, only 94 per cent of the men's (Crow, 1981). Surprisingly, in the US, the wage differential between men and women managers has been shown by one study to be actually worse than the national earnings average. Nationally, women earn 62 per cent of what men earn; women in managerial and administrative jobs earn 60 per cent of what men earn (Brown, 1982). Brown (1982) maintains that in the US part of the problem stems from the kind of low-paying fields of management which women have entered, e.g. food, retail trade, health administration and general office administration.

While it appears easy for women to gain employment at the lower levels of an organization, it is proving very difficult for them to reach upper, middle and senior management positions. Therefore with more women entering managerial positions, as a minority group subjected to male dominated policy making, research findings are indicating that female managers are subjected to a greater number of work-related pressures compared to their male counterparts (Davidson and Cooper, 1980a; Cooper and Davidson, 1982). This is of particular significance when one considers that, first, the job of management has been isolated as being a high stress occupation for males (Cooper and Marshall, 1978; Marshall and Cooper, 1979), and second, that female managers have listed being able to 'cope with pressure' as an important factor contributing to their success (Larwood and Kaplan, 1980).

The specific problems and pressures which have been isolated as being unique to female managers include: burdens of coping with the role of the 'token woman', lack of role models and feelings of isolation, strains of coping with prejudice and sex stereotyping, and overt and indirect discrimination from fellow employees, employers, the organizational structure and climate (Hennig and Jardim, 1979; Crow, 1981; Cooper and Davidson, 1982). These stresses combined with those of trying to maintain a family and/or home, are creating enormous pressures on women in management, which may manifest themselves in a variety of undesirable ways. For example one needs to ask whether or not women who take on full-time careers and those who take on traditionally male jobs, will end up with the 'male diseases of work'. Will they join the growing number of men who suffer from stress-related illnesses as a result of work?

The incidence of stress-related illness continues to grow in the UK in contrast to a reduction in many countries, including the USA and the Netherlands. England and Wales have shown an increase in coronary heart disease for example, of 5.1 per cent over the last decade and Northern Ireland 12.5 per cent. Cooper (1982) maintains that stress-related maladies affect most families and possibly three times more working days are lost because of stress illness than all industrial disputes. Although there are doctors who feel that working women are less at risk than men (*Lancet*, 1980), there are studies in this field which are disturbing. For example, recent evidence from the USA National Heart, Lung and Blood Institute has shown that married working women with children were at substantially greater risk of developing coronary disease than housewives (Haynes and Feinleib, 1980).

What is clear, is that the health of women is changing in the UK, and in the USA. As Wingerson (1981) shows, in both countries, death due to coronary heart disease (CHD) and lung cancer has been increasing since the 1950s. Wingerson also makes the important point that there has been little attempt to include women as a separate category in health research, let alone *employed* women.

With more women entering the male-dominated field of management in Britain, the authors decided that this was an area which required further investigation in order that their pressures, problems and stress outcomes were recognized and tackled. The specific objectives of the study on which this book is based are as follows.

(1) To highlight the major pressures and stress experienced by women in management (including supervisory, junior, middle and senior managers), as described by women managers themselves.

(2) To isolate the major problems and pressures of being a woman as compared to a man manager.

(3) To isolate and compare the major effects of these specific pressures in terms of behavioural and health outcomes between women and men occupying all levels of the managerial hierarchy.

(4) To analyse the relationship between behavioural/ health measures and the demographic and stressor factors that act on female and male managers, i.e. high risk profiles.

(5) To relate the findings to the training needs of women managers and to propose recommendations for changes in corporate and legislative policies in order to minimize some of the pressures and barriers faced by women managers.

CHAPTER 2

Pressures on women managers

What is stress?

Stress is a word derived from Latin and was used popularly in the seventeenth century to mean 'hardship, straits, adversity or affliction'. During the late eighteenth century its use evolved to denote 'force, pressure, strain or strong effort', with reference primarily to a person or to a person's organs or mental powers (Hinkle, 1973).

The concept of stress is not a new one, but it is only since the beginning of the twentieth century that the social and biological sciences have begun investigating the effects of stress on the physical and mental health (well being) of people. In 1910, for example, Sir William Osler assumed a causal relationship between hard work, stress and strain with his patients suffering from 'angina pectoris'.

It was not, however, until the middle 1930s and 1940s with the work of Hans Selye, that these types of phenomena were scientifically investigated as individual manifestations of a single coordinated stress syndrome. Thus, Hans Selye (1946) was one of the first to try to explain the process of stress-related illness with his General Adaptation Syndrome (GAS). The GAS was one of the first indications that the body's adaptability was finite; as under constant stress exhaustion always resulted. The GAS consisted of three stages encountered by an individual in stressful situations.

(1) The *alarm reaction* in which an initial shock phase of lowered resistance is followed by counter-shock during which the individual's defence mechanisms become active.

(2)   *Resistance,* the stage of maximum adaptations and, hopefully, successful return to equilibrium for the individual. However, if the cause of stress continues or the defence does not work, the individual will move on to the third stage.

(3)   *Exhaustion,* when adaptive mechanisms collapse.

Cooper (1981) suggests that these theories of the 1930s and 1940s presented stress as a simple stimulus–response model, whereas today, there is a movement towards viewing it as an interactive process. This interactionist thinking was proposed by Lazarus (1966). He suggests that stress has been used to signify environmental agents which disturb structure and function, as well as response to such agents, and Lazarus asserts that it is the three different emphases – physiological, sociological and psychological – which have influenced the discrepancies in definitional and theoretical approaches in stress research.

Lazarus (1966) has formulated a concept of cognitive appraisal and psychological stress or threat, whereby stress is not seen as an imbalance between objective demand and the organism's response capability, but as an imbalance between *perceived* demand and *perceived* response capability. Psychological stress or threat, therefore, according to Lazarus, implies the anticipating of adverse consequences arising from failure to meet demands – the organism is able to alter the state of stress by: (i) avoiding the consequences, (ii) fulfilling the demands (at a tolerable cost) or (iii) altering the perception of demands or capabilities and/or consequences.

The mental and physical ill-effects of stress are frequently used as measures of stress. Selye (1976) reports that such diseases as psychiatric disturbances, cardiovascular disease and bronchial maladies, as well as diabetes, tuberculosis, migraine and gastrointestinal malfunctions, are all stress-induced. Moreoever, stress can impair the body's immune system, which in turn can make an individual more susceptible to infectious diseases and viral illness (Selye, 1976).

Indeed, stress has been shown to elicit physiological changes releasing adrenal hormones which contribute to a release of increased amounts of fatty acids from adipose tissue (Levi, 1971). These lipid changes, i.e. triglycerides and cholesterol levels, have been associated with and used diagnostically in numerous studies of coronary heart disease (CHD) (e.g. Rosenman, Brand, Sholtz and Friedman, 1976; Carruthers, 1980). Stress has also been found to induce such physiological changes as increased blood pressure and changes in various catecholamine hormones (e.g. thyroxin) in urine and blood (Frankenhaeuser, 1974).

At the behavioural level, there are certain symptoms which have been identified by which stress can be recognized. Cooper (1981) has isolated the following major stress-induced behaviours:

(1) difficulty in thinking rationally and seeing all aspects of a problem;
(2) rigidity of views, prejudice;
(3) withdrawal from relationships;
(4) out-of-place aggression and irritability;
(5) excessive smoking;
(6) an inability to relax, resulting in excessive drinking or a need for sleeping pills.

Furthermore, prolonged stress has, in general, been shown to decrease physical stamina, mental alertness and reaction time. Too little or too much stress has been found to be detrimental to performance (Otway and Misenta, 1980). However, the detrimental effects stress has on performance depends on numerous variables including the personality of the individual, the degrees of stress experienced and the effects of training. Hammerton and Tickner (1968), for example, in their investigation of the effects of stress upon skilled performance in three different levels of practice in parachutists, found that, although anxiety produced a decrement in tasks of this kind, such decrements could be minimized by appropriate training.

The causes of stress

In order to fully understand the sources of stress on female and male managers, it is important to appreciate all the environmental and individual causes of stress. We intend, in this chapter, therefore, to review the literature on the potential sources of occupational stress and subsequent stress outcomes. In particular, we want to highlight the influence of both organizational and extra-organizational factors on the individual at work. Previous research has shown the latter to be most pertinent to women in managerial positions. However, it is important to point out that compared to the number of studies on male managers, there is a scarcity of quantitative research material relating specifically to occupational stress in female managers.

This multidimensional approach acknowledges that stress at work can also affect an individual in her home and social environment, and vice versa. Thus, when isolating the sources and effects of stress in a specific occupational group, i.e. women managers, one also has to be aware of the importance of the extra-organizational sources of stress which can affect the behaviour, performance and the mental/physical health of an individual at work (Davidson and Cooper, 1981a).

Particular emphasis will be placed on specific potential causes of stress in the work environment previously identified by numerous research studies. These will include the discussion of such factors as:

(1)   those intrinsic to the job (including acquiring managerial skills);
(2)   role in the organization (including the role of the 'token' woman);
(3)   relationships at work (including sexual harassment);
(4)   organizational structure and climate (including career development issues);

The two major extra-organizational areas which have been singled out as sources of stress and which the authors intend to review are:

(1)   the home and social environment, e.g. career versus home conflicts; marital/relationship problems, etc.
(2)   the individual differences and determinants, e.g. the 'culture trap'; Type A coronary-prone behaviour patterns, etc.

Finally, a number of potentially detrimental outcomes of stress will be covered. These include behavioural outcomes such as impaired job performance, drug abuse, physical illnesses such as migraine and hypertension, and mental illness.

Sources of work stress

A special emphasis is made on reviewing the literature delineating organizational causes of stress which have been isolated as having particular relevance to women in management. In any job there are a wide variety of potential causes of stress, some of which are common to both men and women, and others which are specific to each group. Since working women tend to suffer from the demands of two or more environments simultaneously, (i.e. home and work), while men are less affected by the home, the everyday responsibilities and demands of the job can be magnified. Indeed the authors' recent survey of 135 senior female executives revealed that almost 70 per cent agreed that the stress they experienced at work was closely related to the basic duties, responsibilities and requirements of the job (Davidson and Cooper, 1980a). The following five major sources of work stress will be discussed: (i) factors intrinsic to the job; (ii) role in the organization; (iii) relationships at work; (iv) career development; (v) organizational structure and climate.

Factors intrinsic to the job

The main sources of stress intrinsic to the job that seem to affect women managers are work overload and underload (feeling undervalued and consequently not being given enough demanding work to do); leadership; having to acquire managerial skills (e.g. being assertive, confident, etc.); and attending or being unable to attend training.

WORKLOAD

French and Caplan (1970) view work overload as being either quantitative (i.e. having too much to do) or qualitative (i.e. being too difficult), and have suggested that this can lead to a range of stress-related illnesses.

Numerous studies have found that women managers are frequently subjected to work overload due to the pressure to work harder to prove themselves against their male counterparts (Larwood and Wood, 1977; Terborg, 1977; Harlan and Weiss, 1980). Indeed, many female managers claim that they have to be better at their job than their male colleagues in order to succeed. This performance pressure has also been attributed to general male attitudes towards women managers, which rest on the assumption that women operate under constraints beyond their control (Terborg, 1977). Furthermore, a 1975 British survey (Hunt, 1975) of management attitudes and practices toward women at work revealed that the majority of men responsible for the recruitment and hiring of employees, hold the view that a woman is likely to be inferior to a man as an employee. Only 43.9 per cent thought it would be a good thing to have more women in senior positions. In fact, Richbell (1976) suggests that an organizational climate of unfavourable attitudes can cause the female manager strain, affecting her personally, causing her to try too hard and too obviously and consequently emerging the worse for wear. Ironically, it seems that women can expect additional support from their superiors if they are perceived as being more competent than a male (Larwood and Wood, 1977).

It has also been suggested that this 'credibility testing' pressure felt by some female managers, combined with feelings of 'being exceptional' or isolated, may induce blocks regarding delegation (Harlan and Weiss, 1980; Harnett and Novarra, 1980). Obviously, inability to delegate work can cause excessive overload. Thackray (1979) reports a recent

American study by Lynch of 100 women executives in which they found that the skill of delegation was the major problem of American women executives.

Job underload, on the other hand, is associated with boring, routine, repetitive and understimulating work environments and has been linked with ill-health (Cox, 1980). For the woman manager in particular, pressures connected with having too little to do can occur in situations such as underpromotion. Women are often steered into managerial directions which offer low ceilings on the managerial hierarchy and/or newly created positions with vague job descriptions and limited power (Langrish, 1981). Although, women are likely to be clustered at the lower levels of most organizations, recent data suggest that male and females perform similarly in managerial positions and have similar degrees of managerial potential (Bartol, 1980; Brown, 1982). Hence, differences in the capabilities and performance of females and males do not constitute likely explanations for the low representation of females in managerial positions.

LEADERSHIP

Women in managerial positions appear to enjoy the leadership role, and there is no evidence to support the contention that women are less efficient managerial leaders than men (Petty and Bruning, 1980). Even so, problems can evolve from a proportion of male and female subordinates who feel uneasy working for a female superior. Apparently, women can be labelled 'bossy' whereas men are labelled 'leaders'. A recent study investigating the responses of male and female managers in American state public human service organizations found a direct relationship between having been supervised by a woman and attitudes toward the motivation of women to manager, (Ezell, Odewahn and Sherman, 1981). The authors suggested that being in direct contact with a woman as a superior may dispel traditional female role stereotypes such as women not being as career orientated as men.

Certainly, dissatisfaction from subordinates can be a

source of stress for superiors and vice versa. Richbell (1976) for example, proposes that women who remain in discriminating organizations, can develop feelings of resentment and become dysfunctional in terms of leadership and the service they provide for their subordinates and clients. Moreover, Larwood and Wood (1979) point out that the frustration or success of a superior is felt acutely by those below her; if a female manager is able to relay her success and confidence to her subordinates, any doubts they have about working for her disappear.

BEING ASSERTIVE AND CONFIDENT

Another potential source of stress for female managers is the pressure to adopt male managerial attributes and skills, such as being more assertive, confident, decisive and delegatory. There is a wealth of evidence that there are very few differences between men and women in cognitive abilities and skills (Reid and Wormald 1982). Sex differences, in cognition, as Blackstone and Weinreich-Haste (1980) have argued, have been overstated and have no physiological basis. Differences within each sex are greater than between sexes. Herbert and Yost (1978) reviewed the relevant literature and concluded that women do possess the qualifications and skills required in management and scientific positions. Nevertheless, due to a combination of socialization and their being members of a minority group, lack of self-confidence and unassertiveness have sometimes been found to be failings of women managers. This can ultimately result in feelings of frustration and stress, as well as hampering career advancement. Research has shown that when asked to describe their strengths and weaknesses, women often begin by describing their weaknesses, and are diffident about their strengths (Paddison, 1981). In a recent review of executive women in America, Christopher Reed (1982) asserted: 'Although tough-minded ambition and determination have transformed the share of top jobs by women in recent years, the outward poise and self-confidence seem often to conceal a woman in need of assurance' (p. 10). He goes on to state that female executives in the US have also been criticized as being 'no better than their male counterparts, slavishly imitating "patriarchal values" of ambition, acquisitiveness and ruthlessness' (p. 10).

Lack of self-confidence also affects ability to delegate: 'delegation seems to be the skill most women executives have trouble developing' (Larwood and Wood, 1977). It appears that women occupying junior management positions are particularly susceptible to problems associated with lack of confidence and assertiveness, compared to their male counterparts (Larwood and Wood, 1977). Fritchie's (1981) report on the training scheme for women co-ordinators in the British food, drink and tobacco industry illustrated how the majority of the women lacked confidence in their own abilities at the beginning of a training course. Even more revealing in terms of restricting women's potential and performance, was the discrepancy found between the desired managerial qualities listed by the women and those proposed by their employers. The personal qualities in managers, highly valued by their employers, included motivation, anticipation, leadership, intelligence, endurance, ambition and decisiveness. Conversely, most of the women believed companies valued enthusiasm, discretion, loyalty, dependability, popularity and industriousness. In another relevant study (Moore and Rickel, 1980), nurses were compared with business women in their style of self-description. The business women were found to be less likely to describe themselves with such adjectives as timid, fearful, uncertain, nervous, passive, etc.

TRAINING

Dissatisfaction with training and inadequate training have been shown to be potential sources of occupational stress for female managers. Indeed, many women in the lower levels of management in Britain lag behind their male counterparts when it comes to the provision of education and training. This is due to a mixture of socialization and lack of opportunities (Wanless, 1981).

The Sex Discrimination Act of 1975 in the UK makes provision in Sections 47 and 48 for 'positive discrimination' in training, but only a handful of educational and training bodies have applied under Section 47. Since women only form about 13 per cent of managers in the UK, management training and development certainly meet the Act's criteria. As Novarra (1981) suggests, the UK's Manpower Services Commission and the Industrial Training Boards are automatically empowered to put on single-sex courses where members of one sex are in a minority in an occupation – and they do not have to seek a special designation from the Department of Employment under the Act. There is some controversy at the moment regarding all-female versus mixed-gender management training courses. Harlan and Weiss (1980) are opposed to all-female management development programmes, arguing that such courses only highlight perceived differences between men and women managers and prove detrimental in the long run. They suggest that there are several reasons for this: (i) women could be seen as deficient in ways that men are not and that they need more training; (ii) women could be seen as receiving 'favoured treatment', which men do not get, and this could increase the alienation and tension between men and women managers. Langrish (1980), on the other hand, argues strongly that research evidence has proved that all-women management groups are less threatening and enable women not to be dominated by the dominant group (men!) in terms of speech, role allocation, loyalty affiliation, risk-taking and need identifications. Certainly, in relation to acquisition of managerial skills, confidence building and assertiveness training, there is evidence that many all-women courses have proved to be successful (Cooper 1981). Langrish (1980) suggests that the arguments against women-only management training programmes are primarily of three kinds.

(1) 'Real world' arguments, that is, if women are going to become successful managers, their training must take place in the real world, alongside men, so that the skills they learn from being with men on courses mirrors the world outside.

(2) The 'special needs' view – to suggest that women have

special needs is to label them as 'different' (i.e. inferior to men).

(3) The 'coping' argument – if women are to learn how to work with men as their superiors, colleagues or subordinates, the best way they can do this is to experience working with them on management courses.

These arguments are relatively weak for the following reasons: (i) male management trainers have a tendency to assign female managers particular roles in a learning community: mother, seductress, pet or iron maiden – roles which restrict the learning potential and experience of the female manager; (ii) the female manager's ability to take risks and develop valuable ways of learning new skills is reduced by the presence of overwhelming numbers of men, who have certain expectations of a woman's role.

As Langrish (1981) indicates, in all female groups, women are more able to admit faults, identify needs and areas of felt inadequacy and engage in interactions which develop their strengths. Harnett and Novarra (1979) agree with this, the 'all-women' courses encourage not only freer interchange of ideas and problems, but also help to build up support groups and networks which mixed groups do not. They go on to say that training for women managers should not merely make them able to cope with 'a man's world' but should help them 'to build the confidence and skills which will enable them to make a proactive and distinctive contribution of their own!'

Role in the organization

A person's role at work has been isolated as a main source of occupational stress, involving role ambiguity (i.e. a lack of clarity about one's job), as well as responsibility for people and conflicts stemming from organizational boundaries (Davidson and Cooper, 1981a; Cooper, 1982). A central pressure point that female managers often experience is their own and others' concept of the female executive, i.e. executive role expectation.

According to Hennig and Jardim (1979) male and female managers can both suffer from role stress if there is an incompatibility between their view of themselves and their definition of the executive role. The complication occurs specifically for the female manager when her perception of the executive role is at variance with that of other managers. As Hennig and Jardim (1979, p. 71) suggest 'it is here, in the bit between others' concept of a particular woman and their concept of the executive role, that the particular woman tends to lose her individuality and to become *any* woman'. Since the executive role is usually perceived by both men and women as fundamentally a male role, any individual woman manager is unlikely to be seen as adequately fitting or meeting the role requirements. Although an individual male manager can suffer from lack of role clarity and role conflict, he does so more on an idiosyncratic basis rather than because *he is a man*. The same cannot be said of women attempting to fulfill exclusively male roles.

Certainly, a proportion of female managers try to cope with this problem by becoming more like male managers. In a recent interview with Betty Friedan, who wrote *The Feminine Mystique,* she said:

I had lunch with a group of women executives, and I was horrified. They were so grim, so bitter, so dressed-for-success. And they told me: 'We have to be hard-headed, like the men, and get rid of all vestiges of femininity.' (Lamb, 1981)

Women managers are also more susceptible to role stress due to the multiple role demands inherent in running a career and a home and family. Larwood and Wood (1979) believe time demands impose a tighter schedule on the personal lives of executive women than on men, the women being less able to relax at the end of the day. Moreover, Ritzer (1977) noted that it was the women in upper levels of the organization who tended to experience significantly greater amounts of 'internal strain', due to conflicting role demands on their time and energy.

THE ROLE OF THE TOKEN WOMAN

Kanter (1977) proposed that if women comprise less than 15 per cent of a total category in an organization, they can be labelled 'tokens' as they would be viewed as symbols of their group rather than as individuals. Also, numerous studies have found that professional and managerial women in token positions experience particular strains and pressures not felt by dominant members of the same organizational status (Terborg, 1977; Kanter, 1977; Harnett and Novarra, 1979; Bartol, 1980). The disadvantages which have been associated with being the token woman, include increased performance pressure, being a test case for future women, isolation and lack of female role models, exclusion from male groups, visibility and distortion of women's behaviour by others in order to fit them into pre-existing sex stereotypes.

Visibility
Harnett and Novarra (1979) believe visibility can lead to loss of privacy and of course to the stresses and strains that go with such a loss. Mistakes are also highlighted, but then again so are successes. While the token woman does sometimes get attention, it is often for her 'discrepant' sex characteristics rather than for her skills which means she has to put extra effort into getting herself taken seriously. Indeed, Kanter (1977) suggests fear of visibility could be a source of fear of success in some women, and the importance of dress is another facet of visibility which women in token positions are particularly sensitive to.

A test case
A particular burden associated with being the token woman are the pressures related to being a test case for the employment of future women in the company at management level. Moreover, Harnett and Novarra's (1979) research findings revealed that the feeling of being a token woman and forever being responsible for representing the entire sex was a continual burden internalized so strongly,

that even being conscious of it and discussing it with one or two other women in similar positions was not adequate for its dispersal. They propose that this cause of stress (along with many others) should be recognized by employers and that the lone or token woman appointee is unlikely to achieve her potential without the social support of other female colleagues.

Isolation and lack of female role models

Women in token positions often complain of feeling isolated and missing female support from other peers. Being a token woman also means often working in an environment which provides no role models of women in senior positions. Numerous studies have shown that female role models in higher managerial positions act as important influences in terms of career aspirations for other women. Fritchie (1981) for example, carried out a survey of women in the food, drink and tobacco industry and found that women are more ambitious if they see other women in positions of influence within companies. Moreover, a large percentage of women in the survey identified one or more female 'models' who had influenced their desire to progress.

ROLES IMPOSED ON FEMALE MANAGERS

Kanter (1977) identifies several stereotypical roles often imposed on women managers: the mother, the confidante, the seductress, etc.

Mother earth

This counsellor role provides an individual from whom one can seek personal counselling and help with personal problems. Bartol (1980) maintains that because the 'mother earth' role requires the female to be passive, nurturant and non-critical, it tends to preclude effective job performance and being taken seriously as a 'manager'. Furthermore, when a woman is placed into the mother/counsellor role by her male superiors, she is often put in a privileged situation as regards personal and organizational confidences, usually denied to her male peers. This in itself, can prove a heavy responsibility (Kanter, 1977).

Pet
In another role alignment the 'pet', the woman becomes a mascot, is expected to stay on the sidelines and is often subjected to patronizing comments or as 'decoration' at meetings with client companies, conventions, head offices, etc., which undermines a woman's self-image and undervalues her competence. According to Bartol (1980), efforts at competence may receive excessive compliments because the efforts are viewed as extraordinary and unexpected. Conversely, efforts to be perceived as routinely competent destroy the pet status but also endanger acceptance.

Seductress
In this role, the female manager is viewed as a sexual object which once again detracts from her credibility as a competent manager. Bartol (1980) refers to recent evidence which suggests that physical attractiveness interacts with sex to produce complex stereotyping even at the managerial job application stage. Unattractive women have less of a chance of getting the job and attractive women tend to be channelled into managerial positions consistent with traditional sex roles. Being labelled seductress is obviously also closely linked with sexual harassment at work (to be discussed later). Also, it hampers a token woman's freedom to work closely with colleagues and socially interact (e.g. business lunch with men at work), without the threat of questioned sexual motivation, innuendo and gossip (Farley, 1980). However, among mature women and those in senior executive positions, sex-role imposition tends to become less an object of focus, as many of the feminine-role components attached to the sex status become less intrusive in interactions between men and women at work (Woolman and Frank, 1975). Ironically, those token women who reject role alignment in order to sustain and establish their competence are often assigned a deviant label such as 'militant feminist', 'iron maiden' and 'man-hater' (Kanter, 1977).

People at work

Relationships at work, which include the nature of relationships and social support from one's colleagues, superiors and
subordinates, have been related to job stress (Cooper and
Payne, 1980).

Studies propose that as a minority group, female managers may face particular difficulties and problems in their
relationships at work. Further, Harlan and Weiss (1980),
emphasize that good working relationships enhance a female
manager's informal training opportunities, which are often
as equally important as formal training. This informal
training can take the form of help, advice, hints, and
suggestions from colleagues, predecessors and mentors.
Nonetheless, they assert that this type of informal training
and development has often excluded women, hence reduc-
ing their opportunities, visibility and skill levels.

In the authors' questionnaire survey of 135 senior female
executives, listed in *Women's Who's Who,* one of the
questions dealt with the level of stress experienced in
working relationships with superiors, peers and subordinates
(Davidson and Cooper, 1980a). Not surprisingly, the highest
degrees of stress were reported in working relationships with
superiors, although the sex of the superior did not appear to
influence the level of stress experienced by the woman.
When asked to compare the levels of stress they experienced
themselves with those they thought were experienced by
others, most of the female executives thought they were
under no more stress than either their peers or their
superiors. Among the minority who thought otherwise, the
gender of the person they compared themselves with was
relevant; at both levels they thought women experience
more stress than men. This finding could be an indication of
extra stresses being experienced by female managers and
their female superiors in comparison with their male counterparts. In addition, of those female senior executives who
thought they were under more stress than other people at
work, most said this was so in relation to their subordinates
(Davidson and Cooper, 1980a).

RELATIONSHIPS WITH SUPERIORS

Potential relationship problems with superiors, particularly relevant for the woman manager, concern being treated differently to male colleagues, the male patron boss and the Queen Bee female boss syndrome.

Being treated differently

For female managers, some of the stresses involved in dealing with male superiors tend to centre around the common assumption that women are poorly qualified, coupled with the finding that in order to gain additional support from their superiors, women have to succeed in being perceived as being more competent than their male counterpart (Larwood and Wood, 1979).

In fact, in the authors' survey of senior female executives, the results indicated that in university and postgraduate degrees, the women were more highly qualified than their male counterparts (Davidson and Cooper, 1980a).

Thus, it would seem women managers not only have to do better at their jobs than their male counterparts, but they are usually better qualified in the first place. Obviously, this also raises questions concerning whether or not women have to be better qualified than men to be appointed to managerial positions in the first place.

The male patron boss

A method which some female managers are developing is the male mentor/patron boss situation, whereby a future manager is informally trained by her immediate superior. Herbert and Yost (1978) emphasize the importance of the male mentor and describe how the mentor develops the managerial skills of his female protégée by giving her progressively more responsible and difficult assignments and positions.

It is of interest to note that a recent American report by Harlan and Weiss (1980) found that the majority of women managers, rather than having one mentor who gave them special help over an extended period, had several short-term mentor relationships which facilitated their advancement. The evidence available (Collins and Ganotis, 1974; Wood, 1975) seems to indicate that most male bosses are supportive of their female subordinates rather than threatened by them, particularly if she is competent and unlikely to jeopardize his relationship with male colleagues. This male boss plays out the 'patron' role, protecting and advancing his protégée, but at the same time using her competence for his own advancement.

Even so, having a male mentor can create enormous stress for the female manager because:

(1)   she feels she must constantly perform at her best to meet his expectations;
(2)   she becomes identified with him and suffers the whims and circumstances that befall him;
(3)   her own individual talents and abilities are not always recognized by 'significant others', but get fused with the boss's strengths and weaknesses;
(4)   she is still playing out a 'dependent role', and not trying to make her mark on the basis of her own resources (Hennig and Jardim, 1979; Cooper, 1982).

Moreover, Brown (1982) in her recent book on American female managers believes that the notion that mentors are important to a woman's career development have been over-emphasized. Indeed, she asserts that the popularity of the mentor concept tends to reinforce the male-dominated organizational status quo.

The female Queen Bee boss

Although a majority of female managers have reasonably good relationships with their male bosses, some who have female bosses are not as content. Miller (1976) indicated that the women who began early to unshackle themselves from their 'fear of power' and other inhibiting traits and attitudes, felt they had to adopt male behaviour patterns. Underneath the facade of the dominant and superordinate style was sometimes a very insecure and less than self-confident and assertive woman. Cooper (1982) suggests this combination of surface behaviour and hidden feelings must have produced in the first generation of senior women managers a rather frightening figure. A woman whose outward behaviour was both determined, aggressive and terrifying to her junior managers (Terborg, 1977).

The concept of the Queen Bee female boss was first posited by Staines, Tavris, and Hayaratne (1973) in which they described the dominant, successful, bossy female senior executive. They suggested the following account of her attitudes and life style:

Other women could succeed in business if they worked as hard as she did. The only way to succeed at executive levels was through individual effort. The Queen Bee had worked hard to attain her position, and she felt 'why should it be easier for others?'. She had a high status job with good pay, and she had achieved social success. She was also eager to succeed in the traditional feminine role of wife and mother. (p. 36)

They also indicated that the Queen Bee was unhelpful to other women, partly because of her desire to remain unique in the organization and because she was fearful of the competition (Staines, *et al.* 1973).

THE THREATENED MALE COLLEAGUE

Many women managers feel that their male colleagues of similar or equal status are competitive, create stress for them and seem to be threatened by them. This takes place particularly at junior and middle management levels, where women still have some opportunity of promotion. It is so, the more competent and competitive the woman is, a combination which in the words of Larwood and Wood (1979) raises the 'masculine consciousness' of her associates who subsequently often exclude her from their social interactions.

Some men feel particularly threatened because they see their organizations increasingly promoting a few women to take up 'token positions' in various departments and levels in the hierarchy (Cooper, 1982). Most men are not 'outwardly' bothered by losing in the promotional stakes to a 'competent woman', but very distressed about a 'less competent' woman achieving success over them (Hennig and Jardim, 1979). It had been assumed that, as the proportion of women increased in organizations, sex bias and the 'threatened male colleague syndrome', would decrease in a linear fashion. However, Harlan and Weiss's (1980) research presents a curvilinear relationship between two variables. That is, a high resistance by male managers to the first women managers in the company followed by a rapid decrease in resistance as the percentage of women managers rises to approximately 10–15; and then a rapid increase in resistance when this percentage increases once more to become large enough to be viewed as powerful and threatening. Moreover, these authors postulate that the speed with which women move into management, combined with the rate of company growth, may be additional variables.

Cooper (1982) suggests that it may be that the more ambitious or achievement-orientated male executives are the ones who will, and are, feeling the most threatened by women who they perceive may have the promotional edge. This may be due to affirmative action (as in America) or equal opportunity legislation and company policy (at least in the lower echelons of organizational life). It may also be that the most threatened is the male manager who fails to achieve success, for one reason or another (lack of competence, being in the wrong place at the right time, or in the right place at the wrong time, etc.). It is of interest to note the results of a recent study of 55 women managers in the US aimed at investigating the effects of equal employment opportunity legislation. Those women who perceived that they were selected for their job because of their sex had less satisfaction with their work, less organizational commitment, less satisfaction with supervision and with their co-workers, and experienced more role conflict and role ambiguity than women who felt their sex was not an important factor in their selection (Chacko, 1982). However, an important intervening variable may have been the negative attitudes of co-workers towards the women who believed they had been given their management jobs because of their sex, i.e. their co-workers also shared the women managers' perceptions.

SEXUAL HARASSMENT

Female managers also have the additional burden of being used or using their sexuality in office politics or career development. The pressure of sexual harassment, such as advances or exploitation, can create serious problems in the work environment. Many women managers do experience some kind of sexual advances from their male colleagues, but Litterer (1976) found that few of them ever had an affair with these men. Moreover, Larwood and Wood (1979) point out that if they did, the outcome could prove disastrous for a woman's long-term career advancement, since traditional sex roles assume women are less able than men.

In the USA, the Equal Employment Opportunities Commission was sufficiently concerned in 1980 to issue guidelines defining sexual harassment as 'unwelcome sexual advances, requests for sexual favours and other verbal or physical conduct of a sexual nature', which take place in a variety of work circumstances. According to the EEOC, employers have a duty to prevent and eliminate sexual abuse and this is backed up by legislation which provides victims of sexual harassment with redress against employers. Even so, American researchers maintain that the majority of women feel that they might be jeopardizing their positions by openly complaining about abusive colleagues.

An extensive recent study on the issue of sexual harassment was carried out by Collins and Blodgett (1981) who surveyed 7,408 subscribers to the Harvard Business Review. They found that about 15 per cent of American men in employment and 42 per cent of women had experienced some form of sexual harassment in the office. Thus, the authors concluded that sexual misconduct in the office is a 'big problem', and can affect the self confidence, morale and efficiency of many workers particularly women. Interestingly, the amount the victim apparently suffers did not necessarily vary with the perceived seriousness of the harassment and many respondents were more distressed by persistent low level misbehaviour.

In Britain, a recent survey by the National Council for Civil Liberties found that more than one in ten working women had felt that a man had been taking advantage of his position at work to make persistent sexual advances to them. Divorced and separated women seemed to be particularly vulnerable. Over a quarter of the sample admitted that they had been the victims of this kind of sexual harassment (National Council for Civil Liberties, 1982).

Cooper (1982) believes that some female managers frequently play games with their male counterparts, as a means of raising their own status, or achieving some immediate decision or advancing their career, or for whatever purpose. These executive women play a variation of Berne's (1964) *Rapo* game (from his book *Games People Play*), which one might call *organizational rapo*. Here the ambitious female manager uses mild flirtation and other feminine ploys to achieve certain jobs, decisions, etc. She may or may not be interested in the man's sexual pursuit, but rather in achieving some career goal or as a method of self-protection, if the target of the flirtation is a senior manager, or to enhance her own esteem among her other colleagues (Cooper, 1982). Although there is little evidence that this sexual role is played very often by female managers, one must be aware of how both male and female managers can utilize sexuality at work – a potentially dangerous game to play.

Career development

The next group of occupational causes of stress is related to career development, which refers to the impact of over-promotion, underpromotion, status incongruities, lack of job security, thwarted ambition, etc. (Cooper and Marshall, 1978; Marshall and Cooper, 1979). Satisfaction with promotional opportunities and salary has been found to be associated with increases in self-esteem and job commitment in management populations (Bhagat and Chassie, 1981). Nevertheless, women generally are still found clustered in low status management and are therefore more prone to the frustrations linked to blocked career development (Thackray, 1979). The reasons isolated as contributing toward this situation include pay, general discrimination and prejudice, blocked promotion and mobility factors, and career tactics.

PAY

Despite the fact that the Equal Pay Act in the UK succeeded in raising the average earnings of women from 65 per cent to 74 per cent of men's wages (from 1970 to 1978), the increase has been slow and has actually declined from 1975 when it was 76 per cent. As Oakley (1980) suggested: 'since women's average gross earnings in Britain are currently some 73.9 per cent of men's, it could be argued that some kind of divine law determines the economic inequality of the sexes'. In addition, nearly 70 per cent of employed women in the UK are in relatively few occupations, including clerical service workers, shop assistants, cleaners, teachers, nurses and textile operatives (Hakim, 1979).

As far as female managers are concerned, they are, by comparison with their male counterparts, poorly paid. They receive about 62 per cent of the average gross weekly earnings of men and those in the 'professions' get only about 73 per cent of male earnings (Wanless, 1981). Although, historically, women in management have been underpaid in the USA, women with university degrees in management are eagerly sought by corporations and are experiencing less pay discrimination than their predecessors. Nevertheless, as Thackray (1979) suggests, as women get closer to the top, male resistance hardens and women are frequently eased out of the mainstream of power to become experts or technicians. Thackray (1979) believes that there are two classes of female executives: *the younger brigade,* who are reaping the benefits of equal opportunity legislation and the women's movement climate; and *the older generation,* for whom little has changed or is likely to. Professor Jennings of Michigan State University found in 1970 that older female managers had pay discrepancies in the order of 35–40 per cent in comparison with their male counterparts. These discrepancies were worse in some industries than others, and less pronounced among the young. But most important of all is the fact that 'companies have learnt to neutralize the equal-pay-for-equal-work demands by juggling and proliferating titles and job descriptions to make comparisons difficult' (Thackray, 1979).

DISCRIMINATION AND PREJUDICE

For most working women, discrimination is a prominent occupational stress factor and indeed every participant in the study of American women executives reported having been discriminated against in some way throughout her career (Hennig and Jardim, 1979). The UK Department of Employment's (1979) investigation of the impact of equal pay and equal opportunities legislation found that there were still a variety of organizational and structural factors which were limiting women's opportunities at work, such as hours of work, geographical mobility, length of service and male-orientated career paths.

Not surprisingly, experience of organizational discrimination were reported by the majority of the authors' senior female executives sample: 74 per cent asserted that over the last ten years in their company, for equally qualified men and women, men had been promoted more rapidly than women. Looking only at the last two or three years about 56 per cent said this was still the case. (Davidson and Cooper, 1980a). Thus while there are indications of some improvement, discrimination appears to still be a major potential cause of stress faced by women in the workforce. While discrimination can lead to stress and disillusionment for some women, others have been found to confront the situation by more careful planning. However, this necessity to manipulate the system more carefully is an additional work pressure for the woman manager, not experienced by her male counterpart to the same degree. Research also indicates that the usual employer attitude – that women are 'poor training and promotional investments' who leave work on marrying and/or starting a family – is particularly detrimental to those who work continuously after marriage and single women who do not marry (Wanless, 1981).

The 1981 Committee on Women's Rights Report at the European Parliament on the conditions of women in Europe conveyed that only 13 per cent of women said they had suffered actual discrimination in the work situation, and only another 13 per cent maintained they thought that women were at any disadvantage to men. However, it was the youngest women in the sample who consistently expressed most discontent concerning personal discrimination. The report also emphasized that the majority of women work exclusively with other women, so direct discrimination is often hidden from them (Toynbee, 1981).

BLOCKED PROMOTION AND MOBILITY

For the few token female managers that are lucky or skilled enough to gain access to the dizzier heights of the executive boardrooms and toilets, the problems of blocked promotion are not important. But for the vast majority of women who are struggling for individual recognition and achievement, the road up the executive ladder is not so easy. They face blockages at all levels, as well as difficulties in the interface between their job and home. Currently, many promotional advances in industry are based on the freedom of managers to be mobile, to move from one site to another, from one area of the country to another, and from one country to another. Indeed, Cooper (1982) maintains one of the chief sources of pressure for the executive family is frequent moving. And, although in many cases, the individuals benefit financially from such relocations, the psychological and social costs to the other members of the family are great. In the UK, it is common for managers to move on average about every two to three years until the age of 50. This may not be much of a problem for single women, but for married female managers, particularly those with children, this is almost impossible (Cooper, 1982).

In the USA, whereas in 1978 only 16 per cent of corporations had developed and offered some type of 'job finding' assistance to the spouses of relocated managers, 30 per cent were doing so by the end of 1979 (Cooper, 1982). Also, American companies are developing a more liberal attitude towards refusal of company moves. In 45 per cent of the firms, the manager could refuse any move without any promotional penalty, 20 per cent felt that refusal of a company move was 'permissible providing the reason was valid', and in only 8 per cent of the companies did they operate a 'one refusal only' policy, i.e. refusal hindered advancement.

Nevertheless, although married women are less likely to be mobile than men, evidence suggests that a single woman in management is not more likely than a man to refuse to be mobile. In fact a recent report by the Industrial Society entitled 'Women in Management – Onwards and Upwards?' (1980) states that as many dual career couples plan their future moves together, firms are reporting that many male managers are increasingly reluctant to change location. Clearly, there needs to be a change in organizational policies regarding job mobility and career advancement for both males and females.

Organizational structure and climate

The final potential source of occupational stress in female managers is related to organizational structure and climate, which includes such factors as restrictions on behaviour, office politics, lack of effective consultation and no participation in the decision-making process (Davidson and Cooper, 1981b).

Richbell's (1976) comparison of male and female managers found that women entering management are often left to their own devices and have to learn their jobs via trial and error, whereas the men are given more direction and support. Richbell (1976) suggests that working in this type of climate of resentment and dissatisfaction, may encourage a woman to adopt such withdrawal tactics as absenteeism, or even quitting the job.

POLITICS, CONSULTATION AND COMMUNICATION

It appears that due to a combination of underdeveloped skills (partly due to socialization and inadequate training opportunities) and deliberate avoidance and exclusion by male co-workers and superiors (previously discussed); women managers can be less effective at managing politics and facilitating effective consultation. One study, for example, compared male and female managers in two companies, and men managers in both organizations reported successfully attempting to get early information about decisions and policy shifts more often than women managers. Moreover, although the men and women in both companies were a part of the informal network, in one company men reported using a broader informal system, including outside contacts and top executives (Harlan and Weiss, 1980).

In particular, women in management often find it difficult to break into the male-dominated 'old boy' network and therefore are denied the contacts, opportunities, policy information, etc which it provides. In fact, there is now a policy movement originating from the USA which advocates networking for women in the professions. Welsh (1980) believes that lack of self esteem is one of the factors which has made women reluctant to use one another professionally (i.e. you need to feel you can one day reciprocate in some way before you can make use of others). Nevertheless, although networking with female contemporaries is a useful support system, until more women gain senior positions in management (especially in Britain), they will still have to learn how to break into the male-dominated networking system, especially in relation to male superiors. After all, politics and networking are bound up with 'power', and unfortunately the power is still held predominantly by men.

Home/work conflict

Although this study aims to investigate and isolate the causes and effects of stress in a specific occupational group, that is, women managers, it is important to be conscious of many of the extra-organizational sources of stress which can affect the mental and physical health of an individual at work. When investigating the disruption of home and social life as a direct outcome of occupational stress, one has to be aware that there is a feedback loop with stresses at work affecting home and social life, and vice versa (Cooper and Marshall, 1978).

It is worth noting that 38 per cent of the authors' sample of female senior executives agreed that the stress they experienced at their job strongly affected their personal life

(Davidson and Cooper, 1980a). As more and more women enter management, they will also have to face the stresses and strains of maintaining their dual managerial roles – corporate manager and family manager. Cooper (1982) argues that this will occur because of the slow moving change in men's attitudes towards female careers. In the short term, this will mean either an increasing number of women staying single or getting divorced, *or* a greater 'real' acceptance by men of the changing role of women and the accompanying social support this will require if women are to work and be involved in extended family life. Of course, organizations themselves could help in this process by providing the support facilities within the work site and in company policy (e.g. acceptance of promotion without mobility, paternity leave etc). (Cooper, 1982.)

The single female manager

In respect to organizational attitude, the married male manager tends to be viewed as an asset, whereas the married female manager is viewed as a liability. On the other hand, the single woman manager, particularly when she reaches the age of 30, is often taken more seriously by her organization (Hennig and Jardim, 1979). Even so, single female managers are subjected to potential stresses at home and work. For those career-orientated women who choose not to marry in their twenties, many seem to experience a certain amount of adverse pressure associated with being labelled as an 'oddity', both at work and socially.

Furthermore, they commonly report incidents of previous broken relationships precipitated by their partner's emphasis on the overriding importance of his career compared to theirs (Cooper, 1982).

Being single and living alone has disadvantages: loneliness, lack of domestic and emotional support, etc. Also, the unattached female manager is more likely to be faced with the pressures and strains linked with having to take care of elderly parents and dependants (Stead, 1978). A final potential cause of stress involves entertaining and socializing, these are important facets of executive life, but ones which are orientated to the couple rather than the single unattached woman. Thus, trying to break into this social network can cause the single female manager additional strain (Cooper, 1982).

The married female manager

Novarra (1980) proposes that the increase in women managers to the same proportion as men managers, will have to come through the employment of married women, including those with children of school or pre-school age. She goes on to suggest that this development also opens up the possibility of a substantial number of part-time managerial posts for both women and men, which: 'will have an interesting, perhaps dramatic effect on the whole, slightly mystical, concept of what a manager is in the Anglo-Saxon countries'. (p. 46)

Nevertheless, in reality, few part-time management jobs exist, and more and more executive women who marry are having difficulty in their dual managerial roles: corporate manager and family manager. Unfortunately, more and more married women managers are either divorcing, limiting their family size, or coping with both worlds at the expense of their physical and psychological health (Cooper, 1980a). Those married female managers who do have children, (especially young children at home) spend more time with their children than male managers do, find themselves less able to relax at the end of the day, and are even more susceptible to feelings of guilt, role conflict, work overload, tiredness and ill-health (Larwood and Wood, 1979; Bhagat and Chassie, 1981).

An interesting observation was made by Pleck (1977) that for men, the work role is allowed to intrude into the family (e.g. dinner delayed because of a meeting), whereas for women the family role is allowed to intrude on the work role (e.g. leaving work early to take care of a sick child). Consequently, according to Gutek et al. (1981), this reverse order of intrusion for the sexes not only places more pressure on the woman but also accounts for some of the negative myths about female workers. Indeed, recent studies both of working women generally, and professional and managerial women in America and Britain, have found that they spend more time on child care and home duties than their husbands (Berk and Berk, 1978; Gutek *et al.* 1981).

Inevitably, a proportion of female managers report relationship and marital conflict or divorce, based on their partner's inability to provide them with adequate support. Contrary to earlier research, recent evidence (e.g. Kavanagh and Halpern, 1977; Bartol, 1980) indicates that there is a strong relationship between job and life satisfaction for females as well as males. Consequently, some professional women are choosing their career, in preference to a male partner who fails to support them in that career. In particular, women managers report that problems often arise when they overtake their husbands in terms of salary and status. It became apparent that some men still view their role of 'breadwinner' as being very important in relation to status and self esteem (Cooper, 1982).

A recent EOC report (1981) notes that in Britain 8.6 per cent of dual earning marriages, the wife earns more than the husband. Indeed Oakley (1980) has questioned how the role reversal of 'breadwinner' has affected the gender relations in marriage as regards money and power. She proposes that it seems that while the better educated husband is 'more likely to concede more rights ideologically than they in fact grant', overall it all depends on 'the pre-existing ideologies of personalities of the actors' – actors being the husband and wife. Certainly, one should consider that women managers themselves may find it hard to cope with a relationship with a lower status, lower paid partner – a man who in their ambitious eyes, could be labelled as 'a failure'. Novarra (1980) advocates that one of the reasons why some men are still unhappy about their wives pursuing an interesting career is that :'they fear the wife's mind will no longer be a blank page on which to scrawl the diary of their day's events because she will have her own burden of problems and frustrations which she wishes to share' (p. 21). However, she believes this is a totally misguided fear which contains a twist of irony in that a woman who has nothing comparable to her husband's work is going to make an unsatisfactory counsellor. In the words of Novarra (1980), rather than women being 'receivers of the psychological waste products' of their husbands' day's works, surely the dual career couple should share the counselling role and work out their own personal strategies?

Stress and personality/culture

One of the major issues in the area of stress research *per se* is the old question, Why are potentially stressful situations perceived as stressful by some individuals and non-stressful by others? Not only are objective social conditions stressful depending upon the perception of the individual subject to it but, Theorell and Rahe (1974) suggest, much of the same sort of stressful condition may manifest as differing types of somatic and psychosomatic responses (e.g. in one person an ulcer, in another migraine).

When investigating stress in female managers, as with any occupational group, one has to be aware that we are still dealing with individuals who will have their own unique life histories; demographic variables (e.g. age, management level, marital status); experiences (including previous training and ability to cope with stress); behaviour patterns and personalities – all of which can be instrumental in determining individual responses to stress.

In the review of specific individual responses to stress, the two main variables will be discussed, which research has identified as being particularly discriminant in relation to individual differences to stressors in female managers: (i) the socialization process or 'the culture trap', and (ii) personality and behaviour, including ability to cope with stress and Type A coronary-prone behaviour patterns.

The culture trap

The 'culture trap' involves sex-stereotyped behaviour and personality attributes which are a potential source of pressure on female managers (Cooper, 1982). It is obvious that a great deal of sex-role learning takes place among women during the early phases of their lives, and that this can translate itself into an attitude of mind that creates difficulties later in working life. This can be called 'the culture trap'. Recent research in the classroom, for example, has found it to be a man's world, where boys get two-thirds of the teachers' attention (even when they are in a minority) and are accustomed to being teachers' pets (Spender, 1982).

Larwood and Wood (1977) describe a number of internal blocks that women experience which derive from early sex stereotyping and socialization. First, many women are caught in the 'low expectation trap', particularly when performing a male-stereotyped task. Women then begin to feel that their abilities are unequal to the requirements of the task, as the inevitable 'vicious circle' widens. And, of course, as Weiner, Nierenberg and Goldstein (1976) have found, the more a person feels her/his ability may not be 'up to' a particular task, for example, managing other people, the lower the likelihood of success. Second, women often also *learn* to fear success. Horner (1970) suggests that many avoid success or 'seeming successful' in order to 'behave in a socially approved manner'. This diffidence or 'fear of success', of course, ends up inhibiting further effort and achievement, and once again we are on the self-fulfilling merry-go-round! Third, women are often socialized not to be assertive or aggressive, or to seek power or control. Fourth, women have been expected, and encouraged, to pursue a *dependent* role *vis-à-vis* men. Some would suggest that this makes them less self-reliant and more amenable to influence.

ASSERTION AND DESIRE FOR POWER

As women are frequently socialized not to be assertive, aggressive or to seek power or control, and since, as McClelland (1975) has suggested, the most successful male managers are the most assertive and have the most highly developed desire for power, women are grossly disadvantaged from the 'pink' cradle of birth. However, Cooper (1982) questions McClelland's premise and suggests that perhaps a different style of management might be even more successful, maybe even a style that is compatible with a more traditional, less aggressive female role. Even so, Cooper (1982) admits that women are most definitely sitting uneasily on the 'horns of a dilemma' when it comes to assertive, power-seeking behaviour. If a woman manager does not display the kind of behaviour that is traditionally associated with successful management (i.e. aggressive, competitive, assertive) then the male managers will feel she is not a very effective manager. On the other hand if she does, many male and female colleagues (as well) will see her as Dipboye (1978) emphasizes, as hostile, maladjusted and overcontrolling, that is, too often 'leadership' qualities for a man are judged as traits of hostility and aggression in a woman.

Christoper Reed (1982) describes how the system is moulding the behaviour of the American female executive:

Matters of protocol and etiquette seem important to the female embryo executive, a field where all the rules were drawn up long ago by men for men. The ritual of the business lunch holds endless fascination, and not a little concern about how to conduct one. A New York advertising agency recently made a market research survey into the subject. The result was a plastic card costing $6.00; Ms Executive presents it to the head waiter before her guests sit down. It reads: 'I am a female executive. I am hosting this party. Please instruct service personnel to address all questions to me. When the bill is presented, I am to receive the check (p.10).

DEPENDENCY

Whereas men have socialized to be independent and career-orientated, women have been encouraged by their parents and peers, the toys and games they are given to play with as children, and the role-taking within the family, to be dependent and nurturant (Cooper, 1982). They are as the nursery rhyme goes 'sugar and spice and everything nice, that's what little girls are made of'. But as Finn, et al. (1969) suggests, constant emphasis on dependency, nurturance, sacrifice and caring, contribute to feelings of ambivalence about self worth. This lack of self confidence and esteem can lead to indecisiveness and low risk-taking, which in the long term can result in low achievement motivation. This whole process can then become a negative circular process, with women avoiding power, fearing success, being indecisive, that is, not being able to cope with the attitudes and behaviours which are an integral part of the managerial process.

Stress-coping ability

The ability to cope with stress is an important aspect of working life, both in terms of work performance and possible illness. In the survey of senior female executives, the majority of the sample believed they coped better with stress than their subordinates of both sexes, and about half of them said they were better able to cope with stress than both their male and female peers (Davidson and Cooper, 1980a). Interestingly, only a third believed their ability to cope with stress was greater than that of their male and female superiors. Also, having control over their work appeared to be an important coping strategy, as 79 per cent of the respondents agreed that stress decreased if they were in control of the situation (Davidson and Cooper, 1980a). It should be added that the results may well have proved somewhat different, had a junior- or middle-level female management sample been surveyed, keeping in mind that senior female managers isolate 'being able to cope with pressure' as an important factor contributing to their success (Larwood and Kaplan, 1980).

Terborg (1977), and Larwood and Lockheed (1979) refer to Hall's (1972) examination of conflicts among working women and methods they used to cope with added stress. Hall uncovered three different coping strategies:

(1)   changing the demands of a role which was termed 'structural role redefinition';
(2)   setting priorities, meeting role demands and otherwise learning to live with the added conflict, which was termed 'personal role redefinition';
(3)   attempting to meet the demands of all the multiple roles which was termed 'reactive role behaviour'.

Generally, 'structural role redefinition' was positively related to satisfaction with one's career, while 'reactive role behaviour' was negatively related to satisfaction (Terborg, 1977). Certainly, married female managers with families who adopt the 'reactive role behaviour' coping strategy in their attempt to meet the demands of all their multiple roles of wife, mother and worker (i.e. the 'superwoman syndrome'), are those most at risk in relation to stress-related maladies.

The Type A manager

The major research approach to individual stress differences began with the work of Friedman and Rosenman (Rosenman, Friedman and Straus, 1964; 1966) in the early 1960s and developed later showing a relationship between behavioural patterns and the prevalance of CHD. They found that individuals manifesting certain behavioural traits were significantly more at risk to CHD. These individuals were later referred to as the 'coronary-prone behaviour pattern Type A' as distinct from Type B (low risk of CHD). Type A was found to be the overt behavioural syndrome or style of living characterized by 'extremes of competitiveness, striving for achievement, aggressiveness, haste, impatience, restlessness, hyperalertness, explosiveness of speech, tenseness of facial musculature and feelings of being under pressure of time, and under the challenge of responsibility'. It was suggested that 'people having this particular behavioural pattern were often so deeply involved and committed to their work that other aspects of their lives were relatively neglected' (Jenkins, 1971). In the early studies, persons were designated as Type A or Type B on the basis of clinical judgements of doctors and psychologists or peer ratings. These studies found higher incidence of CHD among Type A than Type B. Many of the inherent methodological weaknesses of this approach were overcome by the classical Western Collaborative Group Study (Rosenman, et al. 1964; 1966).

An increasingly large number of studies have been carried out which support the relationship between Type A behaviour and ill-health (Caplan, Cobb and French, 1975). From a management perspective the most significant work was carried out by Howard, Cunningham and Rechnitzer (1976). Twelve different companies examined 236 managers for Type A behaviour and for a number of the known risk factors in CHD (blood pressure, cholesterol, triglycerides, uric acid, smoking and fitness). Those managers exhibiting extreme Type A behaviour showed significantly higher blood pressure (systolic and diastolic) and higher cholesterol and triglyceride levels. A higher percentage of these managers were cigarette smokers and in each age group studied, Type A managers were less interested in exercise (although differences in cardiorespiratory fitness were found only in the oldest age group). The authors conclude that Type A managers were found to be higher on a number of risk factors known to be associated with CHD than Type B managers. (Howard, *et al.* 1976). More recently, Burke and Deszca (1982) investigated 75 managers (mostly male) and found Type A behaviour to be significantly related to career outcomes reflecting disappointment, alienation and personal failure.

As with male Type A individuals in the work force, high occupational status also appears to relate to Type A behaviour, especially in working women aged 40 to 59 years (Waldron, 1978). Also, Waldron, Zyzanski and Skekelle (1977) in their study of employed men and women revealed that, unlike men, working women show maximum Type A scores between the ages of 30–35 years, when 'speed and impatience' were exaggerated. These authors advocated that this 'age peak' was due to the fact that more Type B females tend to leave their jobs on having children before the age of 30, and hence, it is the A types who tend to persevere with their careers (Waldron, *et al.* 1977). With 90 per cent of women having at least one child, between the 30–35 year age bracket and working women having one-third less free time than housewives, it is perhaps not surprising that time pressures, overload and impatience become prevalent for working women in this age group (Davidson and Cooper, 1980b). It is also of interest to note that a recent study found that Type B subjects were more aroused during work than during inactivity in terms of catecholomine and cortisol excretion and heart rate, whereas Type As showed a tendency to be equally aroused or even more aroused, during inactivity (Frankenhaeuser, Lundberg and Forsman, 1980). In the same vein, Type As felt more distressed than Type Bs during inactivity. Therefore, the authors suggested that inability to cope with inactivity is yet another factor which may add to the health risk associated with Type A behaviour (Frankenhaeuser, *et al.* 1980).

Bearing in mind these findings, one would expect a sample of women managers to be predominantly Type A individuals. In fact, this proved to be the case in the authors' sample of 135 senior female executives (Davidson and Cooper, 1980a). Of the sample, 61·5 per cent were classified as Type A, with 21·5 per cent Type A1 and 40 per cent Type A2. Only 38·5 per cent could be classified as B3 and there were no B4 people. (The distribution of Type A and B behaviour patterns in the general population tends to be: A1, 10 per cent; A2, 40 per cent; B3, 40 per cent, and B4, 10 per cent.) (Rosenman *et al.* 1964). Thus the sample contained over twice the proportion of the most extreme Type A1 individuals, who are most at risk in terms of stress-related illnesses (Davidson and Cooper, 1980a).

Therefore, one might conclude that in order for women to be successful, they need to be a Type A individual. However, research indicates that Type Bs are just as likely to be as ambitious and intelligent as their Type A counterparts. Moreover, unlike the Type A person, the drive in the Type B is associated with security and confidence rather than irritation and annoyance (Davidson and Cooper, 1980b). Much of the research investigating Type A behaviour in the work setting suggests that stress within the work environment itself enhances Type A behaviour patterns. Rosenman (1978) strongly proposes that when many individuals enter occupations such as switchboard operators, taxi-cab drivers, assembly-line workers, managers and so on, they often do not possess A type patterns of behaviour. But, increased time pressures, demands for speed and conscientiousness required by the job can make a relaxed Type B into a Type A, or a less extreme Type A2 into the more exaggerated Type A1 (Rosenman, 1978). None the less, there is the issue of self-selection which requires consideration, i.e. perhaps Type A women are also more likely to be attracted to managerial positions. Burke and Deszca (1982) studied the relationship of Type A behaviour to organizational climate preferences in 118 male and female students of administration who were about to undertake full-time employment. They found that individuals with higher Type A scores were more attracted to work environments that were compatible with their Type A propensities.

Stress-related illness

Over the past 20 years, the incidence of stress-related illnesses such as coronary heart disease has been on the increase. In 1976 the American Heart Association report estimated the cost of cardiovascular disease in the USA at $26·7 billion a year (Cooper 1980a). In England and Wales the death rate due to coronary heart disease (CHD) in men doubled between 1950 and 1973, and has increased much more rapidly than that of older age ranges (for example, 45–54). Indeed, by 1973, 41 per cent of all deaths in the age group 25–44 were due to cardiovascular disease (Cooper, 1980a). What is of even greater relevance is that there is substantial evidence suggesting that occupational stress is a causal factor in such stress-related diseases as CHD (Cooper, 1981).

Women generally tend to be stronger against disease and death compared to men (Selye, 1976). This is true not only for every infectious agent but also for Western Society's two major causes of death – heart disease and cancer. However, there are indications both in the USA and Britain, that death from CHD and lung cancer is on the increase in women, and the change has been attributed to the increase in women entering the work force and consequently being exposed to 'occupational stress' (Wingerson, 1981). Furthermore, comparing the incidence of duodenal ulcers in women, in 1957 and 1977, for women over 45 years of age, the incidence of perforated duodenal ulcers had increased by almost 40 per cent (Wingerson, 1981).

There are indications that women tend to react differently to stress than do men, whose reactions tend to have more physiological manifestations. Wingerson (1981) describes the research being carried out in Stockholm by Marianne Frankenhaeuser who believes that the male and female responses to stress are learnt and not due to innate biological factors. Frankenhaeuser found female engineering students reacted more like men than like other women in relation to their levels of stress hormones cortisol and adrenalin, during a stressful situation (Wingerson, 1981). Therefore, as in the male-dominated field of engineering, one could hypothesize that women in the masculine field of management may also be prone to eliciting similar stress reactions.

Executive health is a topical issue among occupational health doctors, personnel managers and others responsible for the well-being of people at work. But very little long-term research has been carried out into its nature, extent and causes. One of the first major studies in this field was carried out by Cooper and Melhuish (1980) among a group of nearly 500 male executives over a ten-year period; this study reveals the cost of stress and some of the problems faced by managers in general, many of which apply to women executives as well.

As well as examining the factors in an executive's life associated with coronary heart disease, Cooper and Melhuish (1980) are also attempting to explore character-istics that might be related to emotional and mental ill health. The results so far indicate that when a manager is at risk of mental ill health, a different set of personality and job factors are present.

(1)   The manager, who tends to be of fairly high intelli-gence, is tense, apprehensive and suspicious.
(2)   He works in a situation where there is a high degree of job insecurity (fear of redundancy, lack of promotional prospects, office politics)

The first few years of the research programme suggest then that the ambitious, driving, 'workaholic', preoccupied with meeting deadlines and working in a job or for an organization which places heavy demands on his time and skills, without providing mutual support or concern for his well-being, is a likely case for coronary heart disease. The research also indicates that managers who are more vulnerable to mental ill-health are likely to be more intelligent than average, more suspicious, apprehensive, serious and tense and, most important of all, working for an organization which cultivates job insecurity – that is, a company management structure which is dominated by internal competition rather than mutual support and teamwork (Cooper and Melhuish, 1980).

The female manager

It is important to ascertain to what extent the stresses and strains inherent in being a woman in management will affect the physical and mental health, and overall well being of this female occupational group. According to American studies, professional women tend to have higher self-esteem and better mental health than homemakers of similar educational status, but in comparison they lack relaxation time (Birnbaum, 1975). For some (especially the working wife), the excessive pressure and scarcity of free time can adversely affect 'stress-coping' abilities and result in such mental and physical illnesses as depression, anxiety, high blood pressure and headaches. This, in turn, can lead to behavioural symptoms such as decreased work performance, changed sleeping habits, alcohol, drug and smoking abuse, poor interpersonal relationships with colleagues and occasional absenteeism (Selye, 1976).

Cooper (1980a) proposes that working women may well join the growing number of men who suffer from stress-related illnesses as a result of work. Certainly, there are doctors who feel that working women are less at risk than men (*Lancet,* 1980), and some research indicates that housewives seem more unhealthy than working women. Wingerson (1981) for example, refers to Waldron's examination of 1965–66 figures from national samples in the USA, that housewives had more chronic illnesses – diabetes, heart trouble, ulcers, allergies and cancer – than employed women. She also describes a study by the Metropolitan Life Insurance Company of New York who studied women listed in the 1964–65 edition of *Who's Who,* in America, which found that as with men, the prominent women were considerably longer-lived than average women (with the exceptions of journalists and entertainers) (Wingerson, 1981). However, she poses the relevant question, 'Are women healthier *because* they are at the top, or is it simply that, by a sort of natural selection, only the healthiest women make it?' (p. 719).

Coronary heart disease and physical ailments

Although CHD is generally twice as prevalant in men as in women, some recent research findings are disturbing. For example, Haynes and Feinleib (1980) re-analysed prospective data drawn from the Framingham Heart Study and discovered that working women did not have a significantly higher incidence of CHD than housewives, and their rates were lower than for working men. However, they then analysed the information in terms of married (including divorced, widowed and separated) versus single working women, and found a substantial increase in incidence of heart disease. But, their results were most revealing when they compared married working women with children against those without children. In this case they found that 'among working women, the incidence of coronary heart disease rose as the number of children increased'. This was not the case, however, for women who were housewives; indeed, that group showed a slight decrease with an increasing number of children. Couple these findings with the strong association between Type A behaviour and CHD (along with hypertension etc.) and one could hypothesize that those female managers most at risk are those Type A1 individuals who are married with children.

In the survey of stress in senior female executives, the authors were interested in discovering the health problems which the sample had experienced in the past (Davidson and Cooper, 1980a). Table 2.1 illustrates the percentage of the

TABLE 2.1   WOMEN MANAGERS REPORTING PHYSICAL
AND PSYCHOLOGICAL ILLNESS

Physical	Per-centage	Psychological	Per-centage
Gastric and/or peptic		Anger	35·6
ulcer	4·4	Irritation	60·0
Asthma	2·2	Anxiety	54·4
High blood pressure	9·6	Tiredness	69·6
Migraine	27·4	Low self-esteem	25·9
Eczema	5·9	Depression	23·7
Heart disease	0·0	Tension (neck or back)	42·2
Arthritis and/or		Sleeplessness	34·1
rheumatoid arthritis	8·1	Frustration	34·8
Stroke	0·0	Dissatisfaction with life	
		or job	34·1

Source: Davidson, M. J. and Cooper, C. L.1980a, p. 51

sample who reported having had stress-related physical and psychological symptoms of illnesses.

It is of interest to note that, with the exception of migraine headaches, overall the sample did not report a high incidence of *physical* ill-health. (However, this was a sample of senior female executives, women who according to Wingerson (1981, p. 719) may be 'healthier *because* they are at the top'.) It is relevant to point out that Wilkinson (1980) reports that headaches and migraines cause more lost working days than strikes and is an illness primarily of the young, affecting three times as many women as men. The causes of migraine are numerous and include physical and psychological stress, change of climate, strong artificial lighting, noise, smoking and high blood pressure (Wilkinson, 1980).

Psychological health

Table 2.1 shows that compared to physical ailments, a greater percentage of senior women managers reported having experienced psychological maladies with irritation, anxiety and tiredness being experienced by well over half the respondents. The high level of psychological maladies and migraines reported by the sample may have been enhanced both by stress experienced at work and the limited relaxation periods in their personal life. Indeed, 71 per cent agreed that they felt their physical and psychological health problems were in some way related to the stress they experienced at work (Davidson and Cooper, 1980a).

These findings, which indicate that women managers in senior positions are more prone to psychological as opposed to physical maladies, support previous studies on both male and female white-collar populations. It has been a commonly-held belief that workers who are prone to psychiatric illness tend to have low socio-economic status backgrounds and low educational achievement, and in consequence work in low-skilled occupations (Kasl, 1973; Schuckit and Gunderson, 1973). However, this assumption has recently been challenged by Cooper (1980b) who, in his review of the findings of two large-scale studies of stress and work by Cherry (1978) and by Caplan, *et al.* (1975), illustrates that the incidences of physical ill-health were greater for blue-collar workers than white-collar workers. Furthermore, nervous strain at work was reported by a higher proportion of white-collar and professional workers than of skilled, semi-skilled and unskilled manual workers. Thus, Cooper (1980b) concludes that these results 'May indicate only that white-collar and professional groups differ from blue-collar occupations in their reactions to stress, that is, that the former reflect the pressures of work in mental illness, whereas the latter do so in physical symptoms and illness' (p. 50). Newberry, Weissman and Myers (1979) examined the psychiatric status and social adjustment of a matched group of working married women and housewives drawn from a community sample. They used the Social Adjustment Scale, Gurin's Symptom Check List and the Schedule For Affective Disorders and Schizophrenia. They found that although there was no difference between the two groups on overall psychiatric symptoms, depressive symptoms, diagnosable psychiatric disorders or treatment for an emotional problem in the past year, married women did differ from housewives in their attitudes toward work and the home. Indeed, they found that housewives suffered from greater 'work impairment', feelings of inadequacy, lack of interest and overall work maladjustment than working wives. On the other hand, working wives were found to be more impaired, uninterested and inadequate in respect of their housework compared to their work. This is no doubt due to the low status associated with housework; Oakley (1974) has emphasized that sociology has never viewed housework as work. However, it should be noted that her survey of the housewives' working week revealed that most worked over 70 hours a week compared to the 40 hours standard in industry.

In a study of psychiatric disorders among professional women, Welner, Marten, Wochnick, Davis, Fishman and Clayton (1979) found that women GPs had a significantly higher rate of psychiatric depression than a control, and that women with children were found to have significantly more career disruption than those without children. Indeed, Hall and Hall (1980) suggest that the main source of stress among two-career couples stems from the fact that the number of demands on the partners exceeds the time and energy to deal with them.

Job dissatisfaction and health

Caplan *et al.* (1975) endeavoured to identify the sources of stress among 23 different occupational groups. According to Cooper (1980b), this investigation identified two separate groups of factors reported by white- and blue-collar workers as responsible for job dissatisfaction and ill health. For blue-collar workers, on the one hand, those factors responsible for (ill) health-related behaviours were lack of job complexity, ambiguity about job future, role ambiguity and under-utilization of abilities. Conversely, for the professional and white-collar workers, the three major causes of stress were responsibility for people, job complexity and concentration, and high and variable workload (Cooper, 1980b).

Low morale has been equated with low work-related self-esteem, which has been associated with such job-related factors as qualitative work overload and inadequate support from superiors and co-workers (McMichael, 1978; Kasl,

1978). In addition to stress-related job variables, self-esteem appears to be of significant importance at the individual interface. According to research by Garrity, Soames and Marx (1977), strong self-esteem is a factor associated with individuals who are successful at coping with stress.

Behavioural manifestations of stress

Some women managers suffer from physical and emotional symptoms of ill-health, while others may manifest the stress in behavioural terms, through decreased job performance, increased smoking, the use of drugs, excessive drinking, and marital/relationship breakdowns.

Smoking

Not only is smoking related to incidences of CHD but also it has been found to be associated with neurosis and anxiety (McCrae, Costa and Bosse, 1978), and to be more common in stressful occupations, along with drug abuse (Selye, 1976). Caplan *et al.* (1975), in a survey of 200 male administrators, engineers and scientists, found that an inability to give up smoking was associated with job stress and high levels of quantitative workload. According to Ikard and Tomkins (1973) the reasons why people found it easier to stop smoking under low occupational stress were centred on their diminished psychological tension. Thus, giving up smoking would be difficult for those working in stressful environments, as a cigarette might help them endure the demands put upon them.

In relation to professional women, and women managers in particular, there appears to be a certain amount of conflicting evidence regarding smoking. Wingerson (1981) maintains that women classed as professional and managerial appear to be at least risk from smoking (see table 2.2). She points out that the fall in cigarette smoking over the past ten years has been most pronounced among women in the professional class and almost negligible among women in the lower social classes. Nevertheless, she also makes the important point that these figures must be viewed with

TABLE 2.2 SMOKING

Women aged 16 and over	Percentage who smoke	
	1972	1980
Professional	33	21
Employers-managers	38	33
Intermediate and junior	38	34
Non-manual		
Skilled manual	47	43
Semi-skilled manual and service workers	42	39
Unskilled manual	42	41

Source: New Scientist, 1981, p. 720

caution as it is highly likely that the husband's job is being registered. Indeed, this could well be the case, taking into account that Jacobson (1981) found that female managers in the USA smoke more than their male counterparts and more than women in any other occupational group. As far as women executives were concerned, 42 per cent smoked regularly, as opposed to only 37 per cent of men in similar jobs. By the end of the 1970s, over 8,500 women had died of lung cancer. Jacobson found that although men tended to smoke due to habit or as a method of relaxing, women smoked during periods of stress. Jacobson also reported a controlled study in which men's and women's smoking behaviours were observed during the showing of two films, one horror and one comedy film. It was found that during the horror film, over 75 per cent of the women reached for a cigarette, while only 30 per cent of the men did so, while the reverse findings occurred during the showing of the comedy film.

Divorce

Divorce rates have risen steeply all over the West. Between 1970 and 1979 the divorce rate in England and Wales doubled and on the present trends, one marriage in three will end in divorce in Britain (*Population Trends*, 1982). Moreover, research findings are indicating that the huge rise in the number of women going out to work may well be influencing the rise in divorce rates. Cherlin (1982) refers to studies in America which show that in the areas of the USA where there are better job opportunities for women, fewer women tended to marry. However, Frances Cairncross believes that women's employment does not seem to cause divorce, so much as to make it possible (Cairncross, 1982). Marital difficulties can occur among managerial women because of the conflicts between running both a home and career and lack of support from the husband. In addition, Haynes and Feinleib (1980) also found that working women as a whole experienced more daily stress, marital dissatisfaction and ageing worries, and were less likely to show overt anger than either housewives or men. Indeed, in a review of the research literature on marital adjustment in two-career marriages (Staines, Pleck, Shepard and O'Connor, 1978), a University of Michigan team found that of the 13 important studies, using either a USA national or regional sample, at least all of them showed that marital adjustment was worse for working wives than for non-working ones.

Drugs

Cooper and Melhuish (1980) found about 30 per cent of their male senior managerial sample taking regular stress-relieving drugs. This is far higher than surveys on the general population. Kennedy (1978), for example, found that GPs reported prescribing psychotropic drugs to about 12.5 per cent of their patients. With women tending to be prescribed stress-relieving drugs more often than men, it would be of interest to ascertain whether a higher percentage of female managers take similar drugs, in comparison with their male counterparts.

Alcohol

Margolis et al. (1974) after interviewing more than 1,500 workers in varying occupations in the USA, found a positive relationship between escapist drinking and a number of specific factors causing job stress. Those experiencing high job stress drank more than those experiencing less job stress. Furthermore, Davidson and Veno (1980), in their investigation of stress in the police force, maintained that the presence of high levels of stress, which is linked to stress at work, can encourage some individuals to resort to heavy drinking as a stress-coping technique. What is clear is that alcoholism is on the increase. Admissions to alcoholism units in British hospitals have increased from under 6,000 in 1966, to 8,000 in 1974 (Cooper, 1980b). Deaths from alcoholism have trebled during the period 1965–77, and in recent years admissions to mental hospitals for treatment of alcoholism has doubled for men and trebled for women (Hoyland, 1980).

It has been suggested by Wilsnack (1973), in a study of 28 female alcoholics, that those women who do not have a well-developed sex-role identity are more vulnerable to alcoholism. Indeed, she found that female alcoholics come from a family background which consists of a dominant, unaffectionate mother and a weak, passive father: 'this parental combination in which both parents deviate from normal sex-role behaviour, does not seem favourable for the daughter's development of a secure, positive feminine indentification' (p. 253).

Summary

From our review of the research on occupational stress in women managers, we would propose that as a minority group subjected to male-dominated policy making and work environments, they face additional pressures both at home and work, compared with men managers. It is also clear that a multidimensional approach to research into occupational stress in women managers (at all levels), compared with men managers, is required. This enables the influence of both organizational and extra-organizational causes of stress on the individual, and their effects on behaviour, performance and the mental and physical health, to be examined.

CHAPTER 3

Measuring and evaluating stress among managers

Research methods

We felt it was essential in this study to adopt both a qualitative and quantitative approach to data collection. The qualitative approach took the form of in-depth interviews with women occupying different levels in the managerial hierarchy. The quantitative data was then obtained by formulating a survey questionnaire (see Appendix), based on the analysis of these interviews and previous research findings in the field. As the formulation of the questionnaire was dependent on the data analysis of the interview material, the method and results of the qualitative data collection stage (Phase 1) will be discussed first. This will be followed by a discussion of Phase 2, in which a questionnaire was developed in order to carry out a postal survey of a large number of women managers as well as a proportion of male managers, throughout Britain.

Phase 1: The managerial women interviewed

Interviewing was undertaken to investigate the major sources and levels of stress experienced by women managers, as well as their effective, and not so effective, coping strategies. The in-depth interviews were conducted between February 1980 and February 1981, with 60 female managers throughout England. The subjects were interviewed either at home or at their workplace; each tape-recorded interview lasted over an hour, and covered some of the following areas:

(1)   Potential causes of stress at work;
(2)   Potential causes of stress at home in a social context;
(3)   Personality;
(4)   Health and behaviour.

The interview format was very unstructured at the beginning of the fieldwork, but gradually, as a result of the responses of the interviewees, became more structured. Typed transcripts were made of each tape-recorded interview, in order to aid qualitative analysis. Details of this material can be found in our previous book *High Pressure* (Fontana, 1982).

Tables 3.1 and 3.2 illustrate the demographic details and the educational qualifications of the interview sample of female managers. The author interviewed a total of 60 women, made up of a stratified sample, representative of the proportion of women occupying junior (including supervisors), middle, and senior management positions in Britain at large, i.e. a total of 25 junior managers and supervisors, 20 middle managers and 15 senior managers. The junior managers were made up of both women in supervisory positions and trainee managers, or managers reporting to middle managers. Middle managers were those reporting to senior managers, or to heads of smaller departments, or sub-areas of larger departments. Senior managers constituted female heads of large departments in large organizations, or heads of plants in smaller organizations, reporting directly to Board members or entire work groups.

The sample was taken from a wide cross-section of private and public organizations (both male and female dominated). The women's positions ranged from head of firm and company directors to personnel managers, trainee marketing managers and retail supervisors. The authors contacted personnel officers in selected organizations throughout the country asking them whether they employed a female manager who would be willing to be interviewed as part of the study. The author then contacted by telephone the women managers whose names had been provided by these personnel officers, in order to arrange convenient interview times. Participation throughout the whole study (Phase 1

TABLE 3.1 INTERVIEW SAMPLE:
PROFILE OF THE FEMALE MANAGER

Management level	Sample size	Average yearly income £	Range £
Senior	15	16,800	11,000–50,000
Middle	20	8,000	6,500–11,000
Junior	14	5,800	4,200–7,800
Supervisors	11	6,300	3,600–7,785
Total sample	60	9,175	3,600–50,000

Management level	Mean age (years)	Age range
Senior	47	36–54
Middle	38	23–57
Junior	27	22–42
Supervisors	38	23–59
Total sample	38	22–59

Marital status	Percentage of female managers
Married	47
Remarried	8
Living with someone	5
Single	25
Divorced	13
Widowed	2

Number of children	Percentage of female managers ever married
1 child	21
2 children	19
4 children	2
Percentage of female managers ever married with children	42
Percentage of female managers ever married with children under school age	7

and Phase 2) was on a totally voluntary basis with anonymity and confidentiality always assured.

The average profile of the manager in the interview sample was that of a 38-year-old woman, who was employed

TABLE 3.2   EDUCATIONAL QUALIFICATIONS:
60 FEMALE MANAGEMENT INTERVIEWEES

University degree	Management level (percentage)				Percentage of total sample
	Senior	Middle	Junior	Supervisors	
First degree	47	45	86	18	50
Masters	13	25	—	—	12
PhD	13	—	—	—	3

full time and had tended not to discontinue her working career pattern (even if she had married and had a family). Her average yearly income was over £9,000 and she was likely to supervise, directly or indirectly, well over 400 people.

What women managers said about stress

In order to analyse the data obtained from the interview transcripts, the method of descriptive statistics was adopted in order to give a percentage estimate of responses to items in the sample population.

STRESS INTRINSIC TO THE JOB AND ORGANIZATIONAL STRUCTURE AND CLIMATE

When the sample was asked to what extent they found their job stressful, 92 per cent indicated that they experienced moderate-to-high stress at work.

It can be seen from table 3.3 that work overload was isolated as a leading cause of stress, even though many women acknowledged that much of this was self-imposed. Many felt they were subjected to work overload due to the pressure to work harder in order to prove themselves, and some female managers claimed that they had to be better at their job compared to their male colleagues in order to succeed. When asked what aspects of their job they disliked, those listed most often by the women managers were 'organizational restrictions and climate' (20 per cent) 'work overload' (17 per cent) 'trouble with interpersonal relation-

TABLE 3.3   INTERVIEW SAMPLE:
WORK SITUATIONS FOUND STRESSFUL

Stressful situation	Percentage of total sample
Work overload – too much to do and too little time	35
Deadlines and time pressures	25
Situations over which no control	12
Conflict between work and home/social life	12
Poor interpersonal relationships at work	12
Staff problems/unreliable staff	7
Inadequate supervision/support from above	7
Staff shortages/turnovers	7
Role conflict, e.g. loyalties between staff and superiors	7
Work underload – having too little to do	5
Disciplining	5
Feeling undervalued	5
Discrimination/prejudice *re:* training, promotional prospects, etc.	5
Keeping up with new technology/equipment	5
Tiredness	3
Unclear job role/boundaries	3
Not being assertive enough – finding it hard to say 'no'	3
Inadequate finances/resources	3
Meetings	3
Threatened male colleagues	3
Organizational restrictions and climate	3
Shift work	3
Poor communications/consultation	3
Workload peaks and troughs	2
Not being able to do the job to your fullest ability	2
Sexual harassment	2
Having to rely on other people	2
Travel	2
Politics	2
Having to perform better, as a woman	2
New challenges/risks	2
Redundancy worries	2
Long working hours	2
Equipment failures	2
Job responsibilities	2

ships at work' (15 per cent) 'administration and paperwork'
(13 per cent) and 'disciplining and sacking someone' (10 per
cent) (see table 3.4).

TABLE 3.4   INTERVIEW SAMPLE: JOB DISLIKES

What do you dislike about your job?	Percentage of total sample
Organizational restrictions and climate	20
Work overload	17
Trouble with interpersonal relationships at work	15
Administration and paper work	13
Disciplining and sacking people	10
Routine	7
Deadlines	7
Work underload	5
Trouble with male superiors	5
Staff shortages	5
Poor supervision/management from above	5
Feeling undervalued	5
Peaks and troughs in workload	3
Poor communications	3
Lack of power and influence	3
Inadequate work feedback	3
Personal/social life sacrifices	3
Missing personal communication with people	3
Inadequate training compared to male colleagues	3
Politics	3
Sexual harassment from male boss	2
Financial cuts	2
Poor equipment/machinery	2
Limited promotional prospects	2
Isolation	2
Lack of resources	2
Home/work conflicts	2
Being female and trying to make voice heard	2
Having to be mobile	2
Having to keep up with new developments	2
Shift work	2
Standing on feet all day	2

It is also interesting to note that many of the problem areas for female managers – particularly feelings of lack of confidence, being less assertive, delegating and needing to be liked and respected at work – were found primarily at the junior/supervisory and middle management levels (see table 3.5). Presumably, the higher up the managerial hierarchy one goes, the more one finds women who have coped with

TABLE 3.5   INTERVIEW SAMPLE: CONFIDENCE, ASSERTION
AFFILIATION AND DELEGATION PROBLEMS

| | Percentage of managers | | | | |
	Senior	Middle	Junior	Super- visory	Total sample
Confidence at work					
Lack of confidence never					
been a problem	80	40	36	27	47
Would like to be more					
confident	7	40	36	36	30
Confident now but a problem					
at beginning of career	13	20	29	36	23
Assertion at work					
Lack of assertion never					
been a problem	60	45	22	27	40
Would like to become					
more assertive	33	45	71	73	53
Assertive now, but not at					
beginning of career	7	10	7	—	7
Affiliation needs at work					
Needing to be liked has					
never been a problem	73	55	64	55	62
Needing to be liked has					
been a problem	13	40	36	27	30
Needing to be liked not now					
a problem, but was at					
beginning of career	13	5	—	18	8
Delegation at work					
Do you have a problem					
delegating at work?					
No	80	75	29	36	58
Yes	7	15	64	9	23
Problems at beginning of					
career, but not now	13	10	7	55	18

and mastered these difficulties. These women tend to be
older, maturity linked with higher status often being associated with increased confidence.

On the issue of training, it was found that 22 per cent of
the sample were absolutely against 'female only' training
courses of any kind, believing them to be a form of

discrimination via segregation, arguing that it was too unlike the 'real world' in organizations. Nevertheless, the majority of the sample conceded that 'all-female management training courses probably had benefits, especially for women just beginning a career in management' (see table 3.6).

The data collected from the women manager interviewees supports the contention that foundation stones of social skill training were in the areas of 'confidence building' and 'being more assertive'. In addition, many of the women in the sample said they personally had benefited more by attending 'off company' courses, where they were able to share work experience problems with people from different organizations, as opposed to being constrained within the context of an in-company training programme.

TABLE 3.6   INTERVIEW SAMPLE:
THE TRAINING WE NEED

Type of training	Percentage of total sample
Confidence building	50
Assertion	42
Interpersonal skills	12
General management skills including delegation, disciplining, negotiating	10
Learning to cope with men at work including sex role stereotyping	8
Political awareness	7
Training for men to cope with women	6
Desocializing re: sex stereotyping	5
Leadership	5
Retraining for women entering workforce	3
Personal presentation	3
Power of speech and public speaking	3
Resilience	2
How to do well at interviews	2

The authors asked the interviewees what managerial skills they would like to develop. Table 3.7 lists these major skills broken down by levels in the managerial hierarchy. It seems that senior female managers are more concerned with

TABLE 3.7   INTERVIEW SAMPLE:
TRAINING SKILLS WE WOULD LIKE TO DEVELOP

Senior managers
Managing people generally
How to deal with men at work more successfully
Putting over a less superficial attitude – people often
   don't know if I mean what I say
Keeping up with new technology
Learning not to take on so much
Consulting skills
Skim reading

Middle managers
Dealing with difficult staff, especially men
Assertion skills
Delegation
How to be taken more seriously, as a woman
Disciplining

Junior managers
Being labelled 'the boss'
Assertion and confidence
Delegation
Training abilities and assertion
Managing more people

Supervisors
Finance and budgeting
Economics
Administration
More mechanical training
More technical training

interpersonal skills of managing people, dealing with men at work more successfully, as well as task skills of learning about new technology and being able to retain more information. Middle and junior managers, on the other hand, appeared to want to learn how to cope with their role as a woman manager, dealing with difficult staff (particularly men), delegation, assertiveness, being more persuasive, and supervisory managers seemed to be interested in developing the basic skills of management, such as understanding finance, new technology, administration, etc.

Role in the organization
A main source of stress that female managers often experience is their own and others' concept of the female manager, i.e. executive role expectations. Also, women managers are more susceptible to role stress due to the multiple role demands inherent in running a career and a home and family. Of the women managers interviewed, 62 per cent reported finding it difficult to relax when they arrived home after work.

An ill-defined job role can also facilitate role conflict and stress. It was found that women most susceptible to this situation were those occupying middle and junior management positions, whereas all the senior female executives said they were clear about their job role. Twenty-five per cent of middle managers, 22 per cent of junior managers and 9 per cent of supervisors said they were unclear about their job role and experienced role conflict. Those women in junior and middle management positions who complained of this stressor were often in newly created job title positions and junior management trainee positions. In both cases, lack of role clarity was most severe if they were the first to have held that particular position. Certainly, in some cases the employers had either consciously or unconsciously made no attempt to clarify the women's job role or help monitor and mould her job boundaries. In addition, many female supervisors reported role conflict stemming from their conflict of loyalties between management and their subordinates. They had often been promoted from the shop/factory floor and were no longer 'one of the girls', on the other hand neither were they management.

As shown in chapter 2, if women comprise less than 15 per cent of a total category in an organization, they can be labelled 'tokens', as they would be viewed as symbols of their group rather than as individuals. The disadvantages the authors found associated with the role of the *token woman,* included increased performance pressure, visibility, being a test case for future women, isolation and lack of female role models, exclusion from male groups, and *distortion of the women's behaviour by others* in order to fit them into existing sex stereotypes. In particular, the majority of women interviewees in 'token' positions maintained they had felt isolated and this was a specific cause of stress for women in middle and junior management positions, i.e. 60 per cent and 71 per cent respectively (see table 3.8).

TABLE 3.8   INTERVIEW SAMPLE: ISOLATION

As a woman in management, have you felt isolated and missed having the support/contact with other female peers?	Management levels (percentage)				Percentage total sample
	Senior	Middle	Junior	Supervisors	
Yes	47	60	71	36	55
No	53	25	7	18	27
N/A (e.g. working in female-dominated organizations, having female peers, etc.)	—	15	21	46	18

Relationships at work

Generally, relationships with superiors,(who were predominantly male) were reported to be quite good by the majority of the women manager interviewees. Indeed, 87 per cent of the total sample reported having received encouragement generally from their superiors, and 48 per cent said they had had mentors of some kind who had been influential in their career development. Relationship problems with superiors tended to centre around being treated differently from male colleagues (including being underused and undervalued, discrimination and prejudice) and in a few cases, sexual harassment.

On the other hand, many women managers felt that their male colleagues of similar or equal status were competitive, created stress for them, and seemed to be threatened by them. This was particularly true at junior and middle management levels, where women still have some opportunity for promotion. It may also be that the person who feels most threatened is the unsuccessful male manager.

However, relationships with both male and female subordinates were reported to be generally good. But, there were occasions when male subordinates (particularly if they were older) had difficulty in coping with working for a younger female boss, and quite a few interviewees reported personal difficulties they had encountered with female subordinates who were uncomfortable working for a woman boss, particularly secretaries.

Finally, in terms of relationships at work, it was found that female managers also have the additional burden of being used, or of using their sexuality in office politics or career development. The pressure of sexual harassment, such as advances or exploitation, can create serious problems in the work environment. The incidence of sexual harassment experienced by the women manager interviewees was disturbing. Adopting the definition of sexual harassment used in Collins and Blodgett's (1981) American Survey, table 3.9 shows that 52 per cent of the sample said they had experienced sexual harassment at work – a 10 per cent increase compared to the American findings. As well, women occupying middle and junior level management positions in particular, were more likely to have been victims

TABLE 3.9   INTERVIEW SAMPLE: SEXUAL HARASSMENT

Defining sexual harassment as: 'unwelcome sexual advances, requests for sexual favours and other verbal or physical conduct of a sexual nature', have you ever experienced any form of sexual harassment at work?	Management levels (percentage)				Percentage total sample
	Senior	Middle	Junior	Supervisors	
No	67	35	36	64	48
Yes, from male superiors	—	10	—	—	3
Yes, from male colleagues/ clients	—	25	21	18	17
Yes, from male subordinates	—	—	7	—	2
Yes, from males at all levels of the hierarchy	33	30	43	9	30

compared to senior female executives. It should be emphasized that the majority of women reporting no experiences of sexual harassment at work were either older, or occupying senior positions or working in predominantly female work environments.

Career development
Potential stress at work related to career development included dissatisfaction with promotion, discrimination, thwarted ambition, mobility problems and so on. When the authors asked the interviewee sample of supervisory, junior, middle and senior managers if they had been discriminated against because of their sex, nearly 80 per cent reported experiencing direct discrimination or prejudice at some time in their recent career. When this data was broken down by level, it was interesting to note that only 67 per cent of senior managers and 54 per cent of supervisory staff reported some experience of sex discrimination in hiring, promotion or some other aspect of their work, whereas 95 per cent of the middle and 86 per cent of the junior managers reported these experiences during the previous year or two.

However, 64 per cent of the supervisory level managers felt that being a female manager had distinct advantages (usually because they were supervising predominantly female workers), with no significant disadvantages. The senior managers did not see many disadvantages (7 per cent), or advantages (7 per cent) of being female in a male-orientated or male-dominated job, while middle and junior managers felt there were greater costs (20 per cent and 22 per cent respectively) than benefits (15 per cent and 14 per cent respectively).

The sample of 60 women manager interviewees were asked whether or not their career advancement was dependent on their mobility. Table 3.10 shows that 40 per cent of the female managers were mobile and able to accept job relocation if necessary – the majority of these women were single. However, 23 per cent of the interviewees were not mobile due to spouse's career, family issues, etc., and consequently they were experiencing blocked career advancement.

TABLE 3.10   INTERVIEW SAMPLE: JOB MOBILITY

Are you mobile?	Management levels (percentage)				Per-centage total sample
	Senior	Middle	Junior	Super-visors	
Yes, promotion/advancement not dependent on it	27	25	7	18	20
Yes, promotion/advancement dependent on it	27	15	29	9	20
No, promotion/advancement not dependent on it	40	35	36	36	37
No, promotion/advancement dependent on it	7	25	29	36	23

Because of the obstacles that women face, it has been suggested that there is a need for them to plan their careers carefully. Thus, it was surprising to discover that 50 per cent of women managers interviewed at all levels in the hierarchy had 'never set themselves a career life plan', while only 25 per cent 'set themselves a career life plan' and 25 per cent 'set themselves a career plan only as their career developed'. The more interesting finding, was that *more middle (43 per cent) and junior (27 per cent) managers are planning their career paths than did the current generation of senior managers (13 per cent).*

THE SINGLE FEMALE MANAGER

Of the 45 per cent of the interview sample who were single (including 5 per cent who were living with someone in a relationship), 70 per cent maintained that remaining single had proved a distinct advantage, from a management career point of view. In particular, many of the single female managers reported being taken more seriously by their organization once they had reached 30 years of age. However, a number of single interviewees over 30 years of age did complain of the pressures associated with being labelled an 'oddity', and surviving socially in a couple-orientated society. In addition, for those women living alone, lack of domestic and emotional support at home was often a major stressor. Many of the single women interviewed stated that during their twenties their energies were concentrated on their career development, leaving little time for close relationships. Nevertheless, it was common for the single women in their late twenties and early thirties to mention dilemmas relating to decisions on marriage and child bearing. Finally, a proportion of older single interviewees reported problems associated with looking after sick and elderly dependants with little emotional or financial support.

THE MARRIED FEMALE MANAGER

Interestingly, 47 per cent of the married women manager interviewees maintained that being married had proved a disadvantage to them in terms of their career development and advancement. The disadvantages the women themselves included were role conflict between running a home/raising children and a career, not being geographically mobile, not having enough time to run a home and career, feelings of guilt about not being a good wife/mother, lack of emotional and domestic support from husband, and having to take work home with them.

In the sample of 60 female managerial interviewees, 42 per cent of those who had ever been married had children, 21 per cent had one child, 19 per cent two children, and 2 per cent had four children. Perhaps not surprisingly, only 7 per cent of those ever married had children under school age at the time of the survey. A high percentage (i.e. 47 per cent) of the married managers interviewed, earned more than their husbands. Furthermore, 13 per cent of those women who had higher incomes than their spouses, admitted that this was a prominent factor causing some problems in the marriage at the time of the interview.

The majority of married women manager interviewees (58 per cent), maintained they spent more time on home and child care duties than their husbands (see table 3.11). Moreover, 42 per cent said that it bothered them that they were having to give more of their time and energies to home duties than did their partners. It is not surprising that these women often complained of feeling tired, stressed and guilty, due to the conflict inherent in their attempts to fulfill the roles of both homemaker and career person simultaneously.

TABLE 3.11   INTERVIEW SAMPLE:
SHARING HOME/CHILD DUTIES WITH SPOUSE

How do you share the home/child duties with your husband?	Percentage of married female managers
I do more and it bothers me	42
I do more and it does not bother me	16
We share 50:50	39
He does more	3

The married female interviewees were also asked whose career came first and was most important in their partnerships. Of these, 29 per cent replied that their husband's career was more important (interestingly these were all senior female executives earning more than their husbands), and 66 per cent stated that the importance of their own careers, compared to their husbands, was equal. Finally, surprisingly few women who were interviewed expressed problems associated with feelings of jealousy from their spouses or boyfriends, relating to the amount of time they spent with other men at work. In fact, the source of most jealousy and hostility directed towards the women managers, was from the wives and girlfriends of the men with whom they worked.

THE CULTURE TRAP

The authors were interested in investigating the following characteristics that previous research findings had associated with the female managers' 'culture trap': locus of control, low expectations, fear of success, assertion and desire for power, and the dependent role.

When the women manager interviewees were asked whether they attributed their career achievements to luck (i.e. external locus of control) or their own hard work (i.e. internal locus of control), 70 per cent replied it was due to hard work rather than luck, 18 per cent maintained it was due about equally to luck and their own hard work, and only 12 per cent believed luck had more of a part to play compared to hard work. Therefore, contrary to a number of previous research findings, the majority of the women in management sample were internalizers. That is, *they believed that their achievements were the results of their own actions* – an attitude also common amongst male managers.

It was also interesting to discover that when the women managers were asked: 'I know this is a difficult question but if you had been born male rather than female, do you think you would be working in the job you have now?' 65 per cent of respondents said 'no' and only 35 per cent said 'yes'. The types of professions the majority of women who said 'no' believed they would now be occupying, if they had been born male, tended to be the 'cream' top professions, (predominantly male occupations), e.g. professor, engineer, scientist, pilot, economist, architect, lawyer, etc. Thus, even the most successful of the senior executives interviewed, often believed her 'true' career ambitions had been restricted due to her sex.

In terms of low expectations and fear of success, the majority of women manager interviewees at all levels of the managerial hierarchy tended to have experienced favourable family backgrounds, parental encouragement and learned *not* to fear success. However, the majority of women supervisors who were interviewed (who also tended to come from working-class backgrounds) reported having no desire to climb higher than supervisory level, believing they did not want and probably could not cope with, the added responsibility and power. Furthermore, many of the women interviewed in this phase of the study, particularly at the junior, supervisory and lower middle management levels, reported that their underdeveloped assertion skills could prove a significant source of stress at work.

Stress and health

PHYSICAL AND EMOTIONAL ILL-HEALTH

In order to differentiate physical and emotional ill-health in women occupying different managerial levels, the interview sample were asked, 'In the recent past have you suffered from any of the following due directly or indirectly to work pressures?' (See table 3.12)

TABLE 3.12   INTERVIEW SAMPLE:
PHYSICAL AND EMOTIONAL ILL HEALTH

In the recent past have you suffered from any of the following due directly or indirectly to work pressures?	Management levels (percentage)				Percentage of total sample
	Senior	Middle	Junior	Supervisors	
Tiredness	67	45	72	91	65
Depression	33	35	50	18	35
Anxiety	40	25	21	36	30
Irritability	40	20	29	—	23
Sleep troubles	20	20	20	18	20
Headaches/migraine	13	5	21	27	15
Premenstrual tension	7	5	14	—	7
Over-reacting	—	—	29	—	7
Crying	—	—	7	9	3
Aggression	—	5	—	—	2
Nervous rashes	—	5	—	—	2
Nail biting	—	—	7	—	2

Table 3.12 shows that at all levels of the managerial hierarchy, tiredness was ranked the stress symptom most common to women managers. For junior and middle managers depression came next, whereas for the supervisory and senior managers, anxiety was rated as the second major symptom. Irritability and sleep troubles were also ranked highly by all levels, with the exception of supervisors who suffered more from migraine headaches.

Many of the women managers did not like to admit that they had suffered from some form of stress-related illness or manifestation and had hidden it from their colleagues at work. Moreover, the reason many of the women interviewees seemed to suffer stress-related manifestations at work was related to their lack of control over situations. As one woman manager put it:

I get angry sometimes, although I try not to as people who keep their cool do better than those who don't. You can make your point better if you keep your cool under stress. I do find that it helps if you can withdraw from the problem for a period and come back to it, that's not always possible but it helps. I have a longish journey home and it's easy motorway and not stressful and I use that time a lot to think over things.

There was also a large group of female managers who admitted that although the pressures of work were enormous, they could not afford to be ill and take time off work. On balance, we were surprised at the large numbers of women who only showed minor symptoms of stress from the organizational and home pressures associated with their dual roles. This may be due to their ability to get the job into perspective, as four female managers suggest:

(1) I try very much to leave my job at the office and not to take it home. I am lucky having a young family as I enjoy my daughter. When I am putting her to sleep sometimes I think 'what am I getting so worked up for, this is what life is about, this is what love is about'. Otherwise my husband and I work at it and we have formed games and strategies to cope. If I have had a very stressful day I will say so as soon as I come home 'I've had a very stressful day and I want to talk about it, do you want to talk now or do you want to talk later?' and he will say 'do you want to cook dinner and be on your own, or do you want to put the baby to bed?' Then we will sit down to dinner and he will say, 'OK let's talk about it now' and I do the same for him, and we have worked hard at it.

(2) I go out and have my hair done or go and chat with people in another department. I like the day to be completely full. I regard everything that goes on in the office as impersonal and therefore I act on doing the job and react impersonally. When you get to be personal then relationships fall down and there are some tough situations that I have tried to handle very firmly, I can assure you,

and very strongly . . . Yes, I've always used this strategy, it's a lonely life, you've to be detached, you have to be friendly but still keep that detached pose, which enables you to handle a discipline problem without stress, without being emotional . . . if you get too close to them then it gets much harder.

(3) I am as honest as I can be. I let out anger, but not necessarily to the person responsible. I choose someone who can cope with my anger. I've got my own escape valve, in order for me to survive in the job I do have to have somebody like that . . . a relationship with someone who allows me to do the yelling. I don't pick on the person whose hopes I am dashing.

(4) I've often thought I'd make a dummy model and when things go wrong at work I'd stick pins into it as the Japanese do! At the moment, I cope with stress by using bad language!

BEHAVIOURAL MANIFESTATIONS OF STRESS

Some of the women manager interviewees manifested the stress they experienced in behavioural terms. For example, in the sample of junior (including supervisors), middle and senior managers, over 40 per cent said they smoked an average of 23 cigarettes a day and significantly more during the work week than during the weekend. Of those who smoked, 74 per cent claimed they did so because of work stress and the rest for other reasons (personal crises, habit, etc.). Therefore, a higher percentage of the interview sample smoked than one would have expected, taking into consideration that recent surveys have found 25 per cent of professional women in Britain smoke, compared to 40 per cent of manual workers (*Social Trends,* 1981).

In relation to marital disharmony resulting from conflicts between home and work, many of the women who were interviewed complained of the fatigue and feelings of conflict which result from running both a home and career. Often, they said they received little emotional or domestic support from their husbands.

The authors were surprised at the number of female managers interviewed who took tranquillizers, anti-depressants, sleeping pills, etc. as a means of relieving tension. Of the senior female executives, over 40 per cent had been, or were, currently taking these drugs, which compares with a lower 30 per cent of a recent survey of senior British male executives (Cooper and Melhuish, 1980). At the middle and junior management levels, the numbers of women on valium and other related drugs was nearer the 30 per cent mark. Furthermore, a small proportion of women managers admitted to having an alcohol problem.

Interview analysis: conclusions

The analysis of the qualitative interview data provided not only a rich source of stressors and stress outcomes in women managers, but also highlighted potential *differences* between women occupying different managerial levels. This proved invaluable in terms of the questionnaire survey formulation which was designed for people at all levels of management from supervisors on the factory floor to senior company executives. Thus, pressure associated with standing on one's feet all day could be a cause of stress for the supervisor, whereas frequent business travel is more likely to be a cause of stress for the senior executive.

Phase 2:
Large-scale survey of female and male managers

Phase 2 of the investigation involved the development of quantitative measures in the form of a survey questionnaire. The questionnaire was derived from the interviews and was comprised of health measures and potential work/home pressures.

Stress at work and management/personality orientation
Personal and job demographics
Job and organizational characteristics
Home and social characteristics
Coping ability
Management style
Type A coronary-prone behaviour index

Health measures
Gurin's General Health Questionnaire
Drug use
Cigarette smoking
Alcohol consumption
Job satisfaction
Work performance

Stress at work and management/personality orientation

PERSONAL AND JOB DEMOGRAPHICS

Section A of the questionnaire consisted of items concerning the respondents' personal and demographic details. As part of the demographic details it was important to ascertain the marital status of managers and whether or not they had children, keeping in mind that working mothers often face additional problems and pressures. Besides basic job demographic details, certain items particularly relevant to the manager's sex were included. For example, whether or not the respondent was the first person of their sex to hold their job title may indicate a person having to occupy previously male- or female-dominated management domain. As well, it is relevant to itemize the ratio of male versus female colleagues, and the ratio of males and females in the respondents' organization occupying different levels of the managerial hierarchy. Obviously, the working environment is totally different for a woman manager all of whose colleagues are female, from that of one whose colleagues are male. The items included in Section A were:

Personal demographics
Age
Sex
Marital status
Number of children
Age of children
Number of other dependants
Educational attainments

Job demographics
Job title
Management level
Whether first person to hold job title
Whether first person of your sex to hold this title
Professional qualifications
Number of years in present job
Number of years with present organization
Number of years during lifetime as full-time employee
Total number of organizations worked for
Continuous versus non-continuous work profile
Ever having worked part-time
Number of years break from the workforce
Annual salary
Number of persons supervised
Ratio of male and female colleagues at work
Size of organization
Ratio of males and females in organization occupying
  different levels of the managerial hierarchy

JOB, ORGANIZATIONAL, HOME AND SOCIAL CHARACTERISTICS

Section B of the questionnaire consisted of 65 potential job
and organizational sources of stress and 15 potential home
and social stress factors. The majority of the factors were
derived from the analysis of the interview material coupled
with previous research findings. For the purpose of analysis,
pressure dimensions were scored on a 5-point, Likert-type
scale from 1 (no pressure at all) to 5 (a great deal of
pressure).

The items included in Section B of the questionnaire are
listed below under the following broad sub-category headings: factors intrinsic to the job, roles, token-woman factors,
career development, relationships at work, organizational
structure and climate, and home and social factors.
However, these sub-category headings are not meant to be
exclusive item categorizations, as a number of items could
easily be listed under more than one sub-category. For

example, disciplining subordinates is a factor intrinsic to the job, but also related to relationships at work, as well as to individual differences factors, such as lack of confidence.

Factors intrinsic to the job
Work overload
Work underload
Time pressures and deadlines
Taking my work home
Long working hours
Managing/supervising people
Disciplining subordinates
Sacking someone
Inability to delegate
Keeping up with new technology/equipment
Staff shortages and staff turnover rates
Attending meeting
Shift work
Equipment failures
Administration and paperwork
Having to stand on my feet all day
The amount of travel required by my work
Lack of variety at work
Inadequate supervision
Playing the counsellor role at work
Being 'the boss'
Business travel and staying in hotels alone
New challenges and risks
Too much responsibility
Feeling undervalued

Roles
Clarity of my job role/job duties
Conflicting job demands, loyalties, etc.

Token woman factors
Being visible
Feeling isolated

Lack of sex role models – person of
the same sex in a position above me,
acting as an example
Members of the opposite sex at work try and
force me into behaviours they associate with
my sex, rather than letting me 'be myself'
Feeling I have to perform better at my job
than colleagues of the opposite sex

Career development
Overpromotion – promoted beyond my competence
Underpromotion – employed beneath my competence
I feel my sex is a disadvantage when it comes
to job promotion/career progress prospects
Sex discrimination and prejudice
Inadequate job and training experience
compared to colleagues of the
opposite sex
Colleagues of the opposite sex being
treated more favourably by management
Unclear career–progress prospects
Rate of pay

Relationships at work
Lack of support from superiors
Lack of social support from people at work
Lack of encouragement from superiors
Sexual harassment of a verbal or a physical
nature
Working relationships with male superiors
Working relationships with male colleagues/
peers
Working relationships with male subordinates
Working relationships with female superiors
Working relationships with female colleagues/
peers
Working relationships with female subordinates
Members of the opposite sex seem uncomfortable
working with me because of my sex

I feel uncomfortable working with members of
the opposite sex

Experiencing prejudiced attitudes from members
of the opposite sex at work because of
my sex

Experiencing prejudiced attitudes from members
of the same sex at work because of my sex

I feel uncomfortable on training courses when a
member of the minority sex

Organizational structure and climate
Lack of control in my work environment
Office politics
Lack of power and influence
My beliefs conflicting with those of the
company/organization
Lack of consultation and communication
Inadequate feedback on my work
Poor work environment
Inadequate resources and finances
Redundancy threat

Home and social factors
Having to move with my job in order to
progress in my career
Not being able to move with my job in order
to progress in my career
My spouse/partner's attitude towards
my career
Demands of work on my relationship with
my children
Demands of work on my relationship with
spouse/partner
Earning more than my spouse/partner
Dependents (other than children)
living at home
My career-related dilemma concerning
whether to marry/live with someone

My career-related dilemma concerning
   whether to start a family
Being single, other people sometimes
   label me as a bit of an
   'oddity'
Being single I am sometimes excluded from
   social and business events such as
   dinner parties
Lack of emotional support at home
Lack of domestic support at home
Demands of work on my private/social
   life
Conflicting responsibilities associated
   with running a home and career

Other

COPING ABILITY

In order to measure the degree to which respondents
adopted positive stress-reducing coping strategies, items
from the reliable and validated coping section of the
Conflict/Stress Questionnaire by Steinmetz (1979) were
used. The positive coping strategies included in Section D of
the questionnaire are listed below. The coping dimensions
were scored on a 5-point, Likert-type scale from 1 (Never)
to 5 (Always); the question being 'How often do you use the
following to relax?'

Positive coping strategies
Relaxation techniques
Informal relaxation techniques
Exercise
Talk to someone you know
Leaving work area
Use humour
Other

MANAGEMENT STYLE

Section D also had ten items selected to differentiate between ten different behavioural management styles, identified from previous research findings relating to both male and female managers (Sadler, 1970; Schein, 1975; Denmarke and Diggory, 1976). The management styles are listed below and were scored on a 5-point, Likert-type scale from 1 (Never) to 5 (Always); the question being: 'How often do you adopt the following management/supervisory styles at work?'

Management styles
Flexible
Efficient
Directive
Authoritative
Positive
Sensitive, sympathetic
Consultative, e.g. joint problem solving
Co-operative
Assertive
Dogmatic

TYPE A CORONARY-PRONE BEHAVIOUR INDEX

An adapted version of the Bortner and Rosenman scale (1967) was selected as the measure of Type A behaviour in the questionnaire. This scale was chosen because it was felt to be one of the most widely validated and comprehensive of the Type A coronary-prone behaviour inventories. The authors' adapted scale consisted of 12 items, each with an 11-point rating scale which included items from the four subscale sections: hard driving, job involvement, speed, impatience, and general Type A behaviour.

This inventory yields scores ranging from 12 to 132, the higher scores being indicative of Type A behaviour. Table 3.13 shows Type A behaviour measure that was included.

TABLE 3.13   TYPE A BEHAVIOUR

Could you please circle the number which you feel most closely represents your own behaviour?

Never late	5 4 3 2 1 0 1 2 3 4 5	Casual about appointments
Anticipates what others are going to say (nods, interrupts, finishes for them)	5 4 3 2 1 0 1 2 3 4 5	Good listener
Always rushed	5 4 3 2 1 0 1 2 3 4 5	Never feels rushed (even under pressure)
Can wait patiently	5 4 3 2 1 0 1 2 3 4 5	Impatient whilst waiting
Goes all out	5 4 3 2 1 0 1 2 3 4 5	Casual
Takes things one at a time	5 4 3 2 1 0 1 2 3 4 5	Tries to do many things at once, thinks what he/she is about to do next
Emphatic in speech (may pound desk)	5 4 3 2 1 0 1 2 3 4 5	Slow, deliberate talker
Wants good job recognized by others	5 4 3 2 1 0 1 2 3 4 5	Cares about satisfying himself/herself no matter *what others* may think
Fast (eating, walking, etc.)	5 4 3 2 1 0 1 2 3 4 5	Slow in doing things
Easy-going	5 4 3 2 1 0 1 2 3 4 5	Hard-driving
Hides feelings	5 4 3 2 1 0 1 2 3 4 5	Expresses feelings
Many outside interests	5 4 3 2 1 0 1 2 3 4 5	Few interests outside work

Source: Adapted from Bartner and Rosenman, 1967.

Health measures

The health measures selected to assess the manifestations of stress included a general health inventory, drug use, cigarette smoking, alcohol consumption, job satisfaction and work performance.

GENERAL HEALTH QUESTIONNAIRE

A modified version of the Gurin Psychosomatic Symptom List (Gurin, Veroff and Feld, 1960) was selected as a valid (and suitable for self-completion) measure of psychosomatic health. This scale has been widely used as a stress measure in research (e.g. Myers, Lindenthal, Pepper and Ostrander, 1972). The Gurin scale was specifically modified by Marshall and Cooper (1979) in their large scale, British study investigating the job pressures and satisfactions of male managers.

Respondents were asked to rate each symptom into one of five categories – *never, rarely, sometimes, often* or *always* – based on their behaviour over the previous three months. An overall health score was then calculated, which could range from 25 (extremely good health) to 107 (extremely bad health).

Symptoms

Do you ever have any trouble getting to sleep or staying asleep?

Have you ever been bothered by nervousness, feeling fidgety or tense?

Are you ever troubled by headaches or pains in the head?

Are there any times when you just don't feel like eating?

Are there times when you get tired very easily?

How often are you bothered by having an upset stomach?

Do you find it difficult to get up in the morning?

Does ill health ever affect the amount of work you do?

Are you ever bothered by shortness of breath when you are not exercising or working hard?

Do you ever feel 'put out' if something unexpected happens?

Are there times when you tend to cry easily?

Have you ever been bothered by your heart beating hard?

Do you ever smoke, drink, or eat more than you should?

Do you ever have spells of dizziness?

Are you ever bothered by nightmares?

Do your muscles ever tremble enough to bother you (e.g. hands tremble, eyes twitch)?

Do you ever feel mentally exhausted and have difficulty in concentrating or thinking clearly?

Are you troubled by your hands sweating so that you feel damp and clammy?

Have there ever been times when you couldn't take care of things because you just couldn't get going?

Do you ever just want to be left alone?
Do you feel you are bothered by all sorts of pains and ailments in different parts of your body?
For the most part do you feel healthy enough to carry out the things you would like to do?
Have you ever felt that you were going to have a nervous breakdown?
Do you have any particular physical or health problem?

DRUG USE

In an attempt to assess the degree to which respondents adopted negative stress-induced coping strategies, items measuring drug use were included in the questionnaire. These five items were included in the validated coping section of the Conflict/Stress Questionnaire by Steinmetz (1979). The dimensions were scored on a 5-point, Likert-type scale from 1 (Never) to 5 (Always). The respondents were asked, 'How often do you use the following to relax?'

Take Aspirin
Use tranquillizers or other medication
Drink coffee, Coke, or eat frequently
Smoke
Have an alcoholic drink

In addition, three more question items were included in order to obtain more details regarding respondents' alcohol consumption and cigarette-smoking habits. These items were adapted from those used in the Henley Executive Health Questionnaire (Cooper and Melhuish, 1980). Respondents were asked, 'Over the past year, which of the following best describes your typical drinking habits?' (One drink is a single whisky, gin or brandy; a glass of wine, sherry or port; or half a pint of beer.) Drinking habit categories ranged from *teetotal; an occasional drink; several drinks a week, but not every day; regularly, one or two drinks a day;* or *regularly, three to six drinks a day.*
Concerning smoking, respondents were asked if they had ever smoked, had given up smoking or were currently

smoking. For those who were currently smoking, they were asked to state the number of average cigarettes smoked a day from seven quantity categories ranging from none to five a day, to 40-plus a day.

JOB SATISFACTION

Job satisfaction was measured by using the items taken from the Job Satisfaction Scale used in numerous stress research studies (e.g. Caplan, *et al.,* 1975; Cooper and Melhuish, 1980). Respondents were requested to indicate which of the following two statements best described how they felt about their present job, using a 5-point Likert scale from 1 (Strongly Agree) to 5 (Strongly Disagree):

I feel fairly well satisfied with my present job
I find real enjoyment in my work

WORK PERFORMANCE

The final major category of variables concerning manifestation of stress, involved detrimental effects on work performance. This category included the following 16 work performance measures, the selection of which, was predominantly dependent on material analysed from the qualitative interview data. Using the 5-point Likert scale from 1 (Never) to 5 (Always) the respondents were asked, 'How often do you feel the following at work?'

Unable to use my skills and knowledge
Unable to make decisions
Unable to meet deadlines
Unable to produce a satisfactory quantity of work
Unable to manage/supervise people satisfactorily
Lack confidence in putting forward my point of view (e.g. at meetings)
Unable to be successful
Unable to do my best
Unable to plan and organize work
Unable to influence and persuade people

Unable to 'sell myself' in competitive situations (inadequate self-presentation)
Unable to cope well in conflict situations
Reacting too emotionally when faced with problems at work
Making mistakes
Lack of self-confidence in the ability to do my job.

Summary

The Appendix consists of the final self-administering questionnaire, which incorporates all the measures we have discussed in this chapter. Before administering the questionnaire to the main research sample, it was important t pilot it using a small sample of women managers. Overall, the changes required on the pilot questionnaire based on the feedback from the pilot sample of female managers, were minor.

CHAPTER 4

Profiles of female and male managers

The aim of this chapter is to describe the procedures incorporated in the quantitative data collection of the main sample in this study, along with the demographic details of the main sample. In addition, the statistical packages that were used in the data analysis will be discussed.

How companies were selected for study

The authors' ideal main sample was to consist of a large proportion of female managers in junior, supervisory, middle and senior positions, and a matched smaller sample of male managers. In addition to the different levels of management, the main questionnaire sample aimed to reflect the following four major variables:

(1) a wide range of industries;
(2) small, medium and large companies;
(3) geographical variety;
(4) predominantly male/female organizations.

A random selection of 1,500 organizations throughout Britain was obtained from the following major industrial categories.

Food, drink and tobacco
Chemicals and allied industries
Instrument engineering
Electrical engineering
Vehicles
Metal goods not elsewhere specified

Textiles
Leather, leather goods and fur
Clothing and footwear
Bricks, pottery, glass, cement, etc.
Timber, furniture, etc.
Paper, printing and publishing
Other manufacturing industries
Gas, Electricity and Water
Transport and communication
Distributive trades
Insurance, Banking, Finance and business services
Professional and scientific services
Miscellaneous services
Public administration and Defence

Within each of the major industrial categories listed above, addresses were provided from small (100–499 employees), medium (500–999 employees) and large (1,000 plus employees) organizations. However, overall the majority (i.e. 1,330) were of small companies, with 85 of medium, and 85 of large organizations. This distribution of organizational size being approximately in accordance with recent censuses of industries in Britain, which have shown that about 90 per cent of all manufacturing industries consist of up to 499 employees, 5 per cent with the number of employees between 500 and 999 and the remaining approximate 5 per cent with over 1,000 employees (Report on the Censuses of Production, 1974–75). The package of questionnaires was sent to the Personnel Officers of their companies, each containing a covering letter, seven questionnaires and seven return stamped envelopes.

The covering létter described the aims of the project and requested that the personnel officer distributed the *seven* enclosed questionnaires to persons in their companies occupying the following management levels:

One female senior manager
Three female middle managers
One female junior/trainee manager
One female supervisor

This distribution of management levels was chosen in an attempt to represent the proportion of women occupying different levels of the management hierarchy. As more women tend to be concentrated in the lower levels of management compared to men, it was anticipated that many organizations would not have women occupying senior or middle management positions (or indeed any management levels). Thus, the personnel officers were asked to match the above distribution as far as possible but when this was not feasible, to distribute the questionnaires to women managers at any level. Therefore, although only *two* women managers at junior/trainee and supervisory level were stipulated, compared to three at middle management level, it was anticipated that proportionally more questionnaires would be handed out to women in lower levels of management compared to those in middle levels and even fewer at senior management levels. As it was also important to include a smaller sample of male managers, for comparison, every personnel officer was also asked therefore, to distribute *one* questionnaire to either:

One male senior manager, or
One male middle manager, or
One male junior/trainee manager or supervisor.

A third of the companies were asked for a male senior manager, a third for a male middle manager and a third for a male junior/trainee manager.

How we analysed the data

As we are concerned with ascertaining the differences and similarities between female and male managers, female and male respondents were treated as two separate sub-populations of the main sample throughout the analysis.

Firstly, the application of descriptive statistics allowed for the measures which have been computed from the sample of collected data to give an estimate of responses to items in the population (Robson, 1973). Hence, this permitted the measure of central tendency via the arithmetic mean to be computed for both female and male manager respondents' scores, along with sample percentage distributions and standard deviation (SD) measures to gauge the variability. Therefore, the utilization of descriptive statistical methods allowed comparisons between female and male managers. Secondly, in order to compare the statistical differences between the female and male manager samples in terms of their responses, *t*-tests were used.

The sample

Personal demographic details

Table 4.1 illustrates the personal demographic details of the main sample of female and male managers.

A total of 696 female and 185 male managers returned completed questionnaires. This was considered to be a good response rate taking into account that: (i) a large proportion of organizations who received questionnaire packages did not have women occupying the specified management positions; and (ii) distribution of the questionnaires to respondents was dependent both on the personnel officer and permission from top management.

Although there was no statistical significant difference between the average age of the female and male samples, the female managers' mean age-range was slightly higher than that of the men: 31–35 years and 36–40 years for women, as opposed to between 26–30 years and 31–35 years for men. Only 56·5 per cent of the women managers were married (including those who had remarried) compared to a higher percentage of 74–6 per cent of men managers. *Therefore, like her American counterpart, British women managers are less likely than British men managers to be married. In addition, it is of interest to note that a greater proportion of women managers compared to men managers has been divorced or were separated, i.e. 15·1 per cent of women (including those who had remarried) compared to 8·1 per cent of men.*

Table 4.2 shows the personal demographic variables in

TABLE 4.1 PERSONAL DEMOGRAPHICS OF 696 FEMALE AND 185 MALE MANAGERS

	Females percentage (number)	Males percentage (number)
Age (years)		
Under 25	12·5 (87)	8·7 (16)
26–30	22·0 (153)	18·6 (34)
31–35	17·4 (121)	25·7 (47)
36–40	12·1 (84)	15·8 (29)
41–50	20·8 (145)	20·8 (38)
51–60	14·7 (102)	9·3 (17)
Over 60	0·6 (4)	1·1 (2)
Marital status		
Married	51·6 (359)	70·8 (131)
Remarried	4·9 (34)	3·8 (7)
Living together	8·2 (57)	5·9 (11)
Single	24·0 (167)	14·1 (26)
Divorced or separated	10·2 (71)	4·3 (8)
Widow/widower	1·1 (8)	0·5 (1)
Number of children		
None	63·8 (443)	37·8 (70)
One	13·0 (90)	13·5 (25)
Two	15·0 (104)	31·9 (59)
Three	5·0 (35)	12·4 (23)
Four or more	3·2 (22)	4·3 (8)
Age of children		
All pre-school	6·5 (16)	13·8 (16)
Pre-school and school age	1·2 (3)	15·5 (18)
All school age	24·5 (60)	38·8 (45)
School and post-school age	19·6 (48)	18·1 (21)
All post-school age	48·2 (118)	13·8 (16)
Dependants		
Other dependants (besides children) living at home	8·0 (53)	14·6 (27)
Educational Attainment		
None	23·1 (160)	9·8 (18)
GCE 'O' Level/CSE	21·5 (149)	14·1 (26)
'A' Level/Ordinary National Diploma	14·0 (97)	26·1 (48)
Higher National Diploma or equivalent	7·5 (52)	15·2 (28)
First Degree	23·5 (163)	22·8 (42)
MA/MSc	3·3 (23)	4·9 (9)
PhD	0·6 (4)	0·5 (1)
Other	6·6 (46)	6·5 (12)

TABLE 4.2   PERSONAL DEMOGRAPHICS: SIGNIFICANT
DIFFERENCES BETWEEN FEMALE AND MALE MANAGERS

	Mean	SD	t	P
Number of children (1=none, to 5:		1·1	6·19	<0·000
= four or more)		1·2		
Females	1·71			
Males	2·32			

	Percent-age	Number	t	P
Having no children				
Females	63·8	443	−7·36	<0·000
Males	37·8	70		
Other dependants (besides children) *living at home*				
Females	8·0	55	−2·37	<0·019
Males	14·6	27		

t = statistical difference between means
P = statistical probability

which there were significant differences between female and
male managers. With a smaller proportion of female managers being married, it was not surprising to find that *the
women had on average, a significantly fewer number of
children and were most likely to be childless compared to
their male counterparts.* (See tables 4.1 and 4.2.) *Of those
women managers who had children, the children tended (on
average) to be older (i.e. 48·2 per cent) with children all past
school age compared to only 13·8 per cent of male managers
with children.* (See table 4.2.) However, a significantly larger
proportion (p<·019) of male managers (i.e. 14·6 per cent)
had other dependants (besides children) living at home,
compared to women managers, i.e. 8 per cent. (See table
4.2.)

When comparing the educational attainment of the female
and male managers, it appears that the men have, overall, a
slightly higher level of educational attainment. Only 9·8 per
cent of men managers had no educational qualifications
whatsoever, compared to 23·1 per cent of the women

managers. On the other hand, in relation to university first degree postgraduate attainment, there was minimal difference between the female and male samples (see table 4.1).

Job demographic details

The job demographic details of the female and male managers are presented in tables 4.3 to 4.6. Tables 4.7 and 4.8 illustrate those job demographic variables in which statistically significant differences were found between the female and male executives.

TABLE 4.3   JOB DEMOGRAPHICS OF FEMALE AND MALE MANAGERS

	Females percentage (number)	Males percentage (number)
Management level		
Supervisor	26·9 (182)	7·6 (14)
Junior manager	30·1 (204)	19·0 (35)
Middle manager	28·4 (192)	39·7 (73)
Senior manager	14·6 (99)	33·7 (62)
Annual salary		
Under £4,000	8·9 (61)	1·1 (2)
£4,000–6,000	28·6 (197)	11·9 (22)
£6,000–8,000	29·5 (203)	25·4 (47)
£8,000–10,000	16·1 (111)	26·5 (49)
£10,000–12,000	9·3 (64)	13·5 (25)
£12,000–14,000	3·3 (23)	10·3 (19)
£14,000–16,000	1·5 (10)	5·9 (11)
£16,000–18,000	0·7 (5)	2·2 (4)
£18,000–20,000	1·0 (7)	0·5 (1)
Over £20,000	1·2 (8)	2·7 (5)
Have additional professional qualifications		
Yes	65·4 (453)	43·7 (80)
First to hold job title		
Yes	40·8 (380)	42·3 (77)
First of sex to hold job title		
Yes	65·4 (453)	43·7 (80)

The female sample consisted of 26·9 per cent supervisors, 30·1 per cent junior managers, 28·4 per cent middle managers and 14·6 per cent of senior managers. Therefore, *the majority of the female sample (i.e. 57 per cent) occupied the lower echelons of the managerial hierarchy (i.e. supervisory and junior management positions), which is generally representative of women's position in management in Britain. Conversely, only 7·6 per cent and 19 per cent of the male sample occupied supervisory and junior management positions respectively (a total of 26·6 per cent).* More than twice the percentage of men occupied senior management positions (i.e. 33·7 per cent) compared to the women, and 39·7 per cent of males were in middle management (see table 4.3).

Overall, there was a significant difference between the management level positions held by the female and male managers (see table 4.7). Men were concentrated in the higher levels of management compared to the female respondents. However, it should be mentioned that management categorization level was dependent on the respondent's perception of status, and it is always possible that men *may* have perceived themselves as occupying higher level management positions than their matched female counterparts.

With a greater percentage of the male sample occupying middle and senior management positions than the female managers, it was not surprising to find that the men earned on average, a significantly higher annual salary than the women (see tables 4.3 and 4.7). Overall, female managers earned on average, between £6,000 and £8,000 a year compared to their male counterparts' salary range of between £8,000 and £10,000. Nevertheless, there were strong indications that regardless of management level, men were still earning more than their female equivalents. For example, in the two of the lowest annual salary ranges, (i.e. under £4,000 and between £5,000 to £6,000) in *every* management level category there was a lower percentage of men than women.

Both the female and male samples were taken from a wide cross-section of major industrial categories throughout

TABLE 4.4 JOB DEMOGRAPHICS OF FEMALE AND
MALE MANAGERS

Job title/category	Females percentage (number)	Males percentage (number)
Education	0·9 (6)	
Health Service	0·9 (6)	
Medicine	0·5 (3)	
Personnel	15·0 (98)	8·4 (15)
Marketing/advertising	5·1 (33)	5·0 (9)
Company Secretary	4·1 (27)	1·7 (3)
Research	0·6 (4)	
Property/Estate Agent	0·2 (1)	
Careers advisor	0·2 (1)	0·6 (1)
Psychology	0·2 (1)	
Civil engineer	0·8 (5)	2·8 (5)
Law	0·6 (4)	
Catering	1·7 (11)	
Company Director	1·7 (11)	6·1 (11)
Chemist/pharmacist	1·7 (11)	1·1 (2)
Quality controller	2·3 (15)	0·6 (1)
Accountant	4·6 (30)	7·8 (14)
Wages/accounts	3·2 (21)	1·7 (3)
Plant manager	1·8 (12)	6·1 (11)
Process manager	0·6 (4)	2·2 (4)
Office manager	3·4 (22)	1·7 (3)
Purchasing/buyer	3·4 (22)	2·8 (5)
Shift manager	0·4 (1)	2·2 (4)
Production manager	2·0 (13)	10·1 (18)
Technical manager	1·7 (11)	2·8 (5)
Food technologist	0·3 (2)	
Retailing	0·8 (5)	
Sales	6·9 (45)	0·6 (1)
Export	2·5 (16)	2·8 (5)
Product manager	2·0 (13)	1·1 (2)
Computing	2·6 (17)	3·9 (7)
Security	1·7 (11)	1·1 (2)
Arts: dance/drama/music	4·3 (28)	0·6 (1)
Training officer	2·8 (18)	0·6 (1)
Administration	2·1 (14)	2·2 (4)
Personal assistant	0·9 (6)	1·7 (3)
Finance	0·9 (6)	0·6 (1)
Public Relations	0·9 (6)	3·4 (6)
Commercial manager	0·6 (4)	0·6 (1)
Progress controller	0·3 (2)	1·7 (3)

TABLE 4.4   (continued)

Job title/category	Females percentage (number)		Males percentage (number)	
Inventory manager	8·1	(53)	3·4	(6)
Works manager	0·3	(2)	1·7	(3)
General supervisor	0·2	(1)	2·2	(4)
Specialist	1·1	(7)	2·8	(5)
Headmistress/master	0·8	(5)	0·6	(1)
Communications manager	0·9	(6)		
Analyst	0·2	(1)	1·1	(2)
Trainee	0·5	(3)	0·6	(1)
Foreman	0·5	(3)	0·6	(1)
Travel industry	0·3	(2)	0·6	(1)
Services	0·2	(1)		
Biology	0·3	(2)	0·6	(1)
Design				
Shipping				
Television			1·7	(3)

Britain and their positions ranged from Company Director to Shift Manager (see table 4.4). The highest proportion of females (i.e. 15 per cent) were concentrated in personnel jobs, a high response rate undoubtedly due to the fact that there was a tendency for personnel officers (who are predominantly women anyway) receiving the package of seven questionnaires to 'distribute' one of the questionnaires to themselves. It should be mentioned that a large number of female and male respondents failed to give their specific job title and many gave their job title as 'a manager'. The majority of both female and male respondents were from organizations with under 1,000 employees (i.e. 71·7 per cent and 80 per cent respectively). However, there was a significant difference in relation to company size, with a greater proportion of females working in slightly larger organizations than the male managers. (See tables 4.5 and 4.7.)

Table 4.5 shows that the majority of both female and male respondents worked in companies where there were predominantly men in senior management positions. Furthermore, 47 per cent of the female sample were employed in companies which constituted of predominantly men at all levels of the hierarchy. The majority of both female and

TABLE 4.5   JOB DEMOGRAPHICS OF FEMALE AND MALE MANAGERS

	Females percentage (number)	Males percentage (number)
Company/organization size		
Up to 200 employees	30·0 (205)	37·3 (69)
200–500 employees	28·5 (195)	33·5 (62)
500–1,000 employees	13·2 (90)	9·2 (17)
Over 1,000 employees	28·4 (194)	20·0 (37)
Company gender constitution		
Predominantly women at all levels of hierarchy	0·4 (3)	0·5 (1)
About 50 per cent women and 50 per cent men at all levels of hierarchy	2·7 (19)	1·6 (3)
Predominantly women, with predominantly men in senior management	20·6 (143)	15·1 (28)
About 50 per cent women and 50 per cent men, with predominantly women in senior management	0·3 (2)	33·0 (61)
About 50 per cent women and 50 per cent men, with predominantly men in senior management	29·0 (201)	49·7 (92)
Predominantly men at all levels of hierarchy	47·0 (326)	
Ratio of male and female peers at work		
All female	7·3 (51)	2·2 (4)
Both male and female	7·4 (511)	81·0 (149)
Have no colleagues	0·6 (4)	
All male	18·2 (126)	16·8 (31)
Worked full-time continuously		
Yes	62·4 (432)	82·7 (153)
Ever worked part-time		
Yes	22·8 (159)	6·5 (12)

male respondents had both male and female peers at work (i.e. 73·6 per cent and 81 per cent respectively), with 18·2 per cent of women managers having all male colleagues compared to only 2·2 per cent of male managers working with all female peers (see table 4.5).

Interestingly, while the female sample overall had attained fewer educational qualifications compared to the men, a higher percentage (i.e. 65·4 per cent), had gained additional professional qualifications compared to 43·7 per cent of the male managers. The percentage of the female and male samples who were the first to occupy their specific job title was similar (i.e. 40·8 per cent and 42·3 per cent respectively). However, a significantly higher percentage of women (65·4 per cent) were the first of their sex to hold their particular job title compared to 43·7 per cent of men (see tables 4.3 and 4.8). This is an important factor, keeping in mind that being the first woman to occupy a management

TABLE 4.6   JOB DEMOGRAPHICS OF FEMALE AND MALE MANAGERS

	Females mean scores (SD)		Males mean scores (SD)	
Number of people supervised	37·2	(262·9)	57·8	(136·4)
Number of people supervised Number of years in full-time employment in present job	5·0	(5·5)	5·0	(5·7)
Number of years in full-time employment in own company/organization	8·4	(7·4)	8·4	(7·1)
Number of years in life-time in full-time employment	15·8	(10·0)	18·4	(10·8)
Number of companies/organizations worked for	3·7	(2·4)	3·7	(2·3)
Of those who have not worked continuously, number of years break from workforce	6·1	(5·0)	1·9	(1·1)

position in an organization (especially in a male dominated management environment) can be a potentially high risk situation in terms of pressure.

In addition, the male managers supervised on average more people than their female counterparts (i.e. 57·8 people and 37·2 people respectively): (see table 4.6).

When examining the career profiles of the female and male managers, not surprisingly a significantly higher proportion (i.e. 82·7 per cent) of men had continuous work profiles as opposed to only 62·4 per cent of women. Of those women who had not worked continuously, their average number of years break from the workforce was 6·1, compared to a significantly lower mean of 1·9 years for men (see tables 4.6 and 4.7). Significantly more female managers (i.e. 22·8 per cent) had ever worked part-time, in compari-

TABLE 4.7. JOB DEMOGRAPHICS: SIGNIFICANT DIFFERENCES BETWEEN FEMALE AND MALE MANAGERS

	Mean	SD	t	P
Management level: (1 = supervisor to 4 = senior management)				
Females	2·3	1·0	8·27	<0·001
Males	3·0	0·9		
Annual salary (1 = up to £4,000 to 10 = over £20,000)				
Females	3·2	1·6	7·26	<0·001
Males	4·3	1·8		
Company size (1 = up to 200 employees to 4 = over 1,000)				
Females	2·4	1·2	−2·88	<0·004
Males				
Number of years in life-time in full-time employment				
Females	15·8	10·0	3·12	<0·003
Males	18·4	10·8		
Of those who have not worked continuously, number of years break from workforce				
Females	6·1	5·0	−10·96	<0·001
Males	1·9	1·1		

TABLE 4.8   HOLDING A JOB: SIGNIFICANT DIFFERENCES BETWEEN
FEMALE AND MALE MANAGERS

	Per-centage	Number	t	P
Being first of sex to hold job title				
Females	65·4	453	5·61	<0·001
Males	43·7	80		
Worked full-time continuously				
Females	62·4	432	−6·07	<0·001
Ever worked part-time				
Females	22·8	159	7·44	<0·001
Males	6·5	12		

son to only 6·5 per cent of male managers (see tables 4.5 and 4.8). And, as one would expect, the mean number of years the male respondents had been in full-time employment was significantly longer than their female counterparts, (i.e. 18·4 years and 15·8 years respectively).

However, what was particularly interesting in terms of career pattern demographics were some of the similarities between the female and male managers. For example, both the female and male samples shared the same average 8·4 years in full-time employment in their present organization, and both had been an average of five years in their present job. Similarities in career and job mobility patterns were further confirmed by the finding that both female and male respondents had worked for an average of 3·7 companies/organizations. Thus, these results suggest that women in management are, with the exception of continuous career profiles, possessing surprisingly similar job change patterns as their male counterparts.

Demographic differences and similarities between male and female managers: a summary

When comparing the average profile of the female manager respondent with her average male counterpart, there are a number of overall differences. Firstly, she is likely to be slightly older (31–40 years compared to 26–35 years for men), she is less likely to be married and more likely to be childless, and if she has children, she will have fewer children who will tend to be older. Almost twice the percentage of women managers have been divorced/separated compared to men managers, and male managers are more likely to have dependants (other than children) living at home. In relation to educational qualifications, overall, women managers have lower educational attainments compared to male managers, although there is little difference between the numbers having obtained university first and postgraduate degrees. Conversely, female managers are more likely to be the first of her sex to hold her job title compared with her male counterpart.

When looking at the overall differences in job demographics between women and men managers, the women are more likely to be concentrated in lower levels of management, supervise fewer people and receive on average, lower annual salaries. As well, the average female manager is more likely to be the first of her sex to hold her job title compared to her male counterpart.

Finally, there were overall similarities between the female and male managers in terms of job demographics. Both female and male respondents tended to work in organizations with predominantly men in senior management positions and had male and female colleagues. The majority of men and women managers had tended to have continuous work pattern profiles, although a higher percentage of women had had a break from the workforce and more female managers had at some time, worked part-time. On average, there were no differences in the number of years women and men managers had worked full-time in their organizations or in their present job, and both sexes had worked for the same number of organizations throughout their life-time of full-time employment.

CHAPTER 5

Work, social and personality pressures: differences between female and male managers

This chapter presents the quantitative results obtained from the survey questionnaire concerning the major differences between female and male managers in relation to the work, social and personality pressures they reported.

Factors intrinsic to the job

T-tests were used to identify whether any significant differences existed between the means of stress associated with factors intrinsic to the job (1 = no pressure at all to 5 = a great deal of pressure) in female and male managers. Table 5.1 shows significant differences between the two samples on three variables associated with being in a position of authority i.e. 'managing/supervising people', 'being the "boss"', and 'disciplining subordinates'. In fact, on all of these three variables, male managers found them to be a significantly higher pressure compared to their female colleagues. Certainly, these results seem to dispel any previous suggestions that women managers find it more difficult and stressful to cope with the authority aspects of leadership than do male managers.

However, women managers reported significantly higher pressure compared to male managers on the two variables – 'having to stand on my feet all day' and 'business travel and staying in hotels alone'. 'Travelling and being alone whilst staying in hotels on business' was also a pressure reported by a high proportion of women managers interviewed in the qualitative part of our study.

TABLE 5.1   FACTORS INTRINSIC TO THE JOB: SIGNIFICANT
DIFFERENCES BETWEEN FEMALE AND MALE MANAGERS

	Mean	SD	t	P
Managing/supervising people				
Females	1·8	0·9	2.`8	<0·023
Males	2·0	1·0		
Disciplining subordinates				
Females	1·8	0·9	2·56	<0·011
Males	2·0	1·0		
Having to stand on feet all day				
Females	1·7	1·2	−2·00	<0·047
Males	1·4	0·9		
Being the 'boss'				
Females	1·6	0·9	3·15	<0·002
Males	1·9	1·0		
Business travel and staying in hotels alone				
Females	1·8	0·1	−5·21	<0·001
Males	1·4	0·7		

Token woman factors

Table 5.2 shows three token woman factors for which significant differences between male and female managers were found, with female managers having higher mean pressure scores on all three factors. Nevertheless, the mean pressure scores for both women and men in response to – 'lack of same sex role models; person of the same sex in a position above me acting as an example' – were quite low. However, when the data was broken down by management level, a significant difference was found between the average pressure scores of female junior managers and male junior managers. Therefore, this finding tends to substantiate the authors' qualitative results in which lack of same sex role models was a pressure to which women in junior management were particularly susceptible.

The average pressure score for female managers in

TABLE 5.2   TOKEN WOMAN FACTORS: SIGNIFICANT DIFFERENCES
BETWEEN FEMALE AND MALE MANAGERS

	Mean	SD	t	P
Lack of same sex role models – *person of the same sex in a* *position above me acting as an* *example*				
Females	1·4	0·9	−3·63	<0·001
Males	1·2	0·6		
Members of the opposite sex at *work try and force me into* *behaviours they associate with my* *sex rather than letting me 'be* *myself'*				
Females	1·7	1·1	−9·47	<0·001
Males	1·1	0·5		
Feeling I have to perform better at *my job than colleagues of the* *opposite sex*				
Females	2·3	1·4	−17·78	<0·001
Males	1·1	0·5		

response to the statement, 'Members of the opposite sex at work try and force me into behaviours they associate with my sex rather than letting me "be myself" ' was significantly higher than for men. Indeed, the pressure scores for this item were higher for women than men at every level of the management hierarchy, with the exception of supervisors. Furthermore, female supervisors are often working in predominantly female work environments and therefore are less likely to be forced into sex-stereotyped behaviours by members of the opposite sex.

Finally, the mean pressure score for women in relation to 'performance' pressure was relatively high compared to male managers. In fact, this was the case for women at all levels of management compared to their male counterparts and significant differences were revealed between the average scores of both populations at every managerial level.

Consequently, feeling they have to perform better at their job than colleagues of the opposite sex, is a pressure experienced far more by women than by men managers.

In terms of coping with the pressures of being a 'token woman', a woman recruitment manager suggests the following 'dos' and 'don'ts':

Always reminding oneself that a job however tough should be fun, or enjoyable at least, therefore while attempting to put one's very best into it, not taking it so terribly seriously that one is frightened of making a mistake – this can be a problem especially for a female in a predominantly male area.

Not making a 'thing' of being terribly conscientious, a female tendency, and embarrassing to male colleagues and superiors.

As the first woman on several long-standing all-male committees, playing things in a very relaxed and low key way until I merged with the team. *Then* participating fully.

Always prepared to fight for one's rights if and when necessary, but with fairness and humour, not with intensity.

Being able, consciously, to relax physically and mentally and positively doing it every now and again.

Career development

Table 5.3 illustrates the disturbing finding that in *terms of career development factors, women managers reported significantly higher pressure scores on four questionnaire items related to sex discrimination and prejudice.* The highest average pressure scores for the female managers were for two items: (1) 'colleagues of the opposite sex being treated more favourably by management'; (2) 'I feel my sex is a disadvantage when it comes to job promotion/career progress prospects.' This was reflected by a senior woman research and development executive:

Having worked for the same firm for 17 years, I have risen steadily in the organization until I now occupy a responsible, reasonably well-paid position. Being a woman the need to keep this job has increased, as I believe I should find it more difficult to find an equivalent position than a man.

Although discrimination exists in our organization (most of the men probably don't even realize this), it can work to my advantage as most men are 'gentlemen' and are often more likely to help me over any difficulty than to lose their temper as they might with a male colleague. However, I have always tried to solve managerial problems myself, perhaps more so than a man, as I feel any failure is likely to be put down to 'feminine weakness'.

In addition, the plight of women managers was highlighted by one of the senior male managers:

In all manufacturing industries women tend to be pushed to one side. I have some strong feelings about why, the majority of which

TABLE 5.3   CAREER DEVELOPMENT: SIGNIFICANT DIFFERENCES BETWEEN FEMALE AND MALE MANAGERS

	Mean	SD	t	P
I feel my sex is a disadvantage when it comes to job promotion/career progress prospects				
Females	2·4	1·4	−23.84	<:0·001
Males	1·0	0·2		
Sex discrimination and prejudice				
Females	2·1	1·2	−14.3	<0·001
Males	1·2	0·5		
Inadequate job and training experience compared to colleagues of the opposite sex				
Females	1·7	1·1	−9·74	<0·001
Males	1·1	0·4		
Colleagues of the opposite sex being treated more favourably by management				
Females	2·2	1·4	−15·25	<0·001
Males	1·2	0·5		
Rate of pay				
Females	2·2	1·2	2·27	<0·023
Males	2·4	1·1		

may (and probably do) relate to company/male attitudes. However, females do carry some of the blame!

As far as equality of opportunity for female managers in the area of training and job experience is concerned, it also appears that women are 'losing out' compared to their male colleagues. The average pressure score for female respondents to the question 'inadequate job training experience compared to colleagues of the opposite sex' was significantly higher than for men.

Average pressure scores for 'rate of pay', however, were significantly higher for men than for women managers. This in itself is an interesting finding, as it suggests that although women in management tend to earn *less* than men, their rate of pay causes them somewhat less pressure. It appears, therefore, that female managers seem to be slightly more satisfied with 'their lot' in terms of pay, even though 'their lot' tends to be less than men in their own professions.

Relationships at work

On seven independent variables dealing with relationships at work, female respondents were under significant pressure in contrast to men. (See table 5.4.) Once again, questions dealing with prejudice yielded significantly higher scores from women managers: 'experiencing prejudiced attitudes from members of the opposite sex at work because of my sex', 'experiencing prejudiced attitudes from members of the same sex at work because of my sex', etc. While the average pressure score for the latter item for women respondents was not high in comparison with men, the result does indicate that a proportion of women managers are being subjected to prejudiced attitudes from other women they work with, whether it be from female subordinates, colleagues or superiors. This prejudice can emanate from various sources, as a senior female manager reflects with respect to her boss:

Even though I face problems because I am a female doing a job previously done by a man, I try not to think about it constantly. If I

TABLE 5.4   RELATIONSHIPS AT WORK: SIGNIFICANT DIFFERENCES
BETWEEN FEMALE AND MALE MANAGERS

	Mean	SD	t	P
Lack of social support from people at work				
Females	1·5	0·9	−2·38	<0·018
Males	1·3	0·7		
Lack of encouragement from superiors				
Females	2·1	1·2	−3·07	<0·002
Males	1·8	1·1		
Sexual harassment				
Females	1·5	1·0	−7·42	<0·001
Males	1·1	0·5		
Members of the opposite sex seem uncomfortable working with me because of my sex				
Females	1·3	0·7	−7·99	<0·001
Males	1·1	0·3		
Experiencing prejudiced attitudes from members of the opposite sex at work because of my sex				
Females	2·0	1·2	−15·03	<0·001
Males	1·1	0·4		
Experiencing prejudiced attitudes from members of the same sex at work because of my sex				
Females	1·6	1·0	−11.75	<0·001
Males	1·1	0·3		
I feel uncomfortable on training courses when a member of the minority sex				
Females	1·5	0·9	−4.29	<0·001
Males	1·2	0·6		

stop trying to show people I can do as well as a man, but just do
the job to the best of my ability, the point seems to go home
better. It is very difficult dealing with a boss who is constantly

trying to analyse me, e.g. do I do things because I am making a decision as a *woman* would? He does not say they are the wrong decision but that I am constantly influenced by thinking as a woman.

This can create problems for the new executive woman in terms of what she should do, as this woman middle manager suggests:

As a woman, I am aware of the advantages of using 'feminine wiles' of the 'little girl' rather than 'sexually alluring' type – but at the same time dislike it myself and am quick to criticize colleagues' sexist remarks about others. Altogether a confusing area, when I justify my attitude by noting that I can't use the old boy network or the chat over a pint method of cementing working relationships. And it works to counterbalance the disadvantages of other types of sexist attitudes which cause one's views to be dismissed. In other words, get ahead by whatever method. Not very satisfying.

Overall, reported pressure associated with sexual harassment (of either a verbal or physical nature) was not particularly high for women at work. As one might expect, however, average pressure scores for women were higher than for men at every level of the management hierarchy, other than the supervisory level (where women tend to work in predominantly female environments). The problem of sexuality at work is reflected by a female middle manager:

The most annoying thing I find is, when having to visit or work in close contact with a male colleague, the rumour or insinuation that you are having an affair, this does not apply to men: if two guys go out for a drink, nobody accuses them of being gay.

'Lack of social support from people at work' and 'lack of encouragement from superiors' were associated with higher levels of pressure by women than men. Certainly, these causes of stress can have detrimental effects on women, both in terms of hampered career development and overall job stress. Average pressure scores for women and men were low in response to the statement 'Members of the opposite sex seem uncomfortable working with me because of my sex'. However, female managers reported greater pressure than male managers on the question of 'feeling uncomfortable on training courses when a member of the minority sex'.

Finally, one can safely assume that being in the male-dominated field of management, a far greater proportion of female respondents will have actually experienced being the minority sex on training courses. The results indicate that this is so.

Home and social factors

Tables 5.5 and 5.6 show the home and social factors in which significant differences exist between the average pressure scores for female and male managers. On all nine items, women managers reported significantly higher stress than men managers. These results, therefore, substantiate previous research findings (e.g. Larwood and Wood, 1979; Davidson and Cooper, 1980a) that women managers, compared with men managers, are far more susceptible to additional extra-organizational stress linked to their home and social environment.

The highest level of stress for female rather than male executives concerned 'my career-related dilemma concerning whether to start a family'. Clearly, this is a major source of pressure for women managers who by the age of 30 are often beginning to establish themselves in their careers and yet at the same time are reaching the 'older primate' years in terms of child-bearing. 'Conflicting responsibilities associated with running a home and career' was the next highest source of stress reported by women. As one woman manager suggested:

I have taken maternity leave and when I returned to work I found that the only way for 'success' at work was to be highly organized, both at home and in the office. A reliable registered baby-minder is essential so that once at work there are no worries about 'baby' until it is time to pick him up. Although my husband helps out to some extent at home, he avoids many of the traditional female roles. I make it a policy not to talk about 'baby' at work

TABLE 5.5 HOME AND SOCIAL FACTORS: SIGNIFICANT
DIFFERENCES BETWEEN FEMALE AND MALE MANAGERS

	Mean	SD	t	P
Earning more than my				
spouse/partner				
Females	1·8	1·2	−7·78	<0·001
Males	1·1	0·5		
Dependants (other than children)				
living at home				
Females	1·7	1·2	−4·60	<0·001
Males	1·1	0·4		
My career-related dilemma				
concerning whether to marry/live				
with someone				
Females	1·7	1·2	−2·39	<0·019
Males	1·4	0·9		
My career-related dilemma				
concerning whether to start a				
family				
Females	2·5	1·5	−9·65	<0·001
Males	1·3	0·7		
Lack of domestic support at home				
Females	1·9	1·3	−5·85	<0·001
Males	1·4	0·8		
Conflicting responsibilities				
associated with running a home				
and career				
Females	2·2	1·2	−6·91	<0·001
Males	1·6	0·8		
Lack of emotional support at home				
Females	1·6	1·1	−3·01	<0·003
Males	1·4	0·8		

which helps in maintaining a more professional status with male
colleagues.

I never refuse or make excuses for attending courses or staying
away overnight as I feel the first time I do this the 'male'
contingent of the company will make a meal of it and thus

jeopardize any chances of promotion in the future, so again an understanding and reliable husband and baby-minder is essential on these occasions.

This finding appears to support the authors' qualitative results, which highlighted the fact that women managers living with a partner do far more when it comes to running a home and a family, which produces greater workload, tiredness, etc. In addition, the female respondents reported greater stress from the 'lack of domestic and emotional support at home' than their male counterparts (see table 5.5).

As indicated in the qualitative study 'earning more than my spouse/partner' was a significantly greater stress for women managers and is undoubtedly related both to problems of adjustment by the woman's partner as well as her own conflicts. Since we found that a high proportion of single female managers we interviewed in Phase 1 tend to be taken more seriously than the married woman manager, it is not surprising that single female respondents reported higher pressure scores in their 'career-related dilemma concerning whether to marry/live with someone'. On the other hand, one single woman indicated that the problems were not only about relationships:

As a single home-owner (with a car and a garden), I work an average 50-hour week at the office and take work home. I compete with male colleagues who, whilst working the same hours, enjoy clean clothes, prepared meals, clean homes and have someone at home to let in the gas man, decorators, repair men, etc. We tend to assume that the main problems facing women in management are the demands of the family/spouse. Believe me, being single and having a career is no push-over!

Even so, although a significantly higher percentage of male manager respondents had dependants (other than children) living at home, women managers recorded higher pressure scores in comparison with men in response to this issue. This indicates that having a dependant living at home means extra work for the woman, in contrast to the male manager, particularly if she is single.

TABLE 5.6 HOME AND SOCIAL FACTORS: SIGNIFICANT
DIFFERENCES BETWEEN FEMALE AND MALE MANAGERS

	Mean	SD	t	P
Being single, other people *sometimes label me as a bit of an* *'oddity'*				
Females	1·8	1·2	−5·93	0·001
Males	1·2	0·5		
Being single, I am sometimes *excluded from social and business* *events such as dinner parties*				
Females	1·7	1·1	−3·75	0·001
Males	1·3	0·5		

Finally, as concluded in Phase 1 of the study, stress factors associated with remaining single are more pronounced in women managers than in men. Table 5.6 illustrates that females reported significantly higher pressure scores to the two items dealing with being single: 'Other people sometimes label me as a bit of an oddity' and 'I am sometimes excluded from social and business events such as dinner parties'. In particular, the latter can prove especially detrimental for the single woman manager who is more prone to exclusion from the business social network. Not only are there more unattached women than men managers (who are more likely to be married), but socially, single men are often viewed as an 'asset' compared to the 'lone female'. And what of the plight of the single parent, female manager?

My male boss was moved sideways and a new job was created for him (it was not possible to sack him) in March 1981. I was offered his job which I naturally accepted. The next few weeks were horrendous and I frequently felt on the point of a nervous collapse. I felt overwhelmed with the burden of responsibility and the powerful sense that all the men in senior positions were cynical about my ability to do any better at managing a department with a long history of problems than my predecessor. The pressure on me seemed enormous and I could not sleep. Having always defined myself as a person who could take responsibility (I was an only child of a divorced parent and became a single parent myself at the age of 21), I was shocked at my own physical and psychological reactions.

But once I got over it I began to feel better than ever before in my life. I felt that this was where I was always meant to be – at the top! I am now much calmer and self-possessed in social situations than ever before in my life.

I consciously try not to overwork though I frequently take work home with me. But I don't always do it! Not having any intimate relationships I tend to put too much emotional energy into my work and become hyperactive. I plan Monday's work on Sunday night. However, I am aware that I make life difficult for others if I overwork and I don't want to appear tense and neurotic. Sometimes I long for someone to talk to and someone to relax with. I have no release at home because it would be wrong to burden my 16-year-old son with my worries and he has his own adolescent problems to contend with.

I think it is important to get out of the building at lunch time. I hate eating sandwiches in the office. But I rarely drink at lunchtimes as it incapacitates me for the rest of the day. I love going to the cinema, exhibitions and the theatre but lack of money, tiredness and dislike of going out alone (although I quite often go out with my son) mean I do not go out very much.

Positive coping strategies

Overall, female and male managers were very similar in their use of positive coping strategies in order to relax. Women managers, however, indicated that they 'talked to someone they knew' as a method of dealing with stress, more often than male executives.

The relaxation strategies used most often by both women and men managers were 'exercise' and 'leaving the work area and going somewhere' (e.g. time out, sick days, lunch away from the organization, etc.). On the other hand, the least popular measures were informal relaxation techniques (i.e. taking time out for deep breathing, imagining pleasant scenes) and relaxation techniques such as meditation and yoga.

Management style

When examining the differences between women and men in relation to the frequency with which they adopt different management/supervisory styles at work, some interesting results emerge. Table 5.7 illustrates that while a significantly greater number of male managers maintained they most often used a *flexible* management style at work in contrast to their women colleagues, women managers maintained they adopted an *efficient* style of management more often than men.

In addition, female managers overall, reported using more frequently the *sensitive* and *sympathetic* style, as well as the *cooperative* approach compared to male managers. Certainly, these results lend support to previous research findings (e.g. Schein, 1975) in the field of leadership behaviour, which have tended to emphasize women's *relationship-orientated* leadership style. Nevertheless, it should be mentioned that significant differences between

TABLE 5.7 MANAGEMENT STYLE: SIGNIFICANT DIFFERENCES
BETWEEN FEMALE AND MALE MANAGERS

How often do you adopt the following management/ supervisory styles at work?	Mean	SD	t	P
Flexible				
Females	3·8	0·8	2·02	<0·044
Males	3·9	0·6		
Efficient				
Females	4·1	0·7	−2·43	<0·015
Males	4·0	0·8		
Sensitive, sympathetic				
Females	3·8	0·8	−3·13	<0·002
Males	3·6	0·8		
Co-operative				
Females	4·2	0·7	−2·91	<0·004
Males	4·0	0·7		

sexes in terms of how often they used different management styles at work, were found in only four of the ten supervisory styles. No significant differences were found in the following management orientation: directive, authoritative, positive, dogmatic, consultative or assertive approaches. In particular, the authors were surprised to find that the mean frequency scores for women and men managers in response to assertiveness were exactly the same.

This appears to contradict previous findings, as well as the authors' qualitative results, which implied that women managers appear less assertive at work in contrast to male executives. In fact, the management styles most often adopted by both women and men managers were the *cooperative, positive* and *efficient* styles. One woman supervisor on the shopfloor described her dilemma and problems with regard to management style:

Most of my work is involved in supervising fitters, etc, on site and since, on the whole, they are more experienced and older than myself I feel unable to use an aggressive style of management. I tend to encourage an avuncular attitude and find that this gives a pleasant working relationship and does not detract from the respect which they feel for me. Younger male subordinates I have no problems with, but have encountered a high degree of resentment and 'bitchiness' from *some* older female subordinates, occasioned mainly by the acceptance and familiarity I have with my male colleagues and superiors.

As far as management style is concerned, one senior woman manager feels that there are certain guidelines a woman should follow:

Ability to be flexible – allow work plan to be interrupted if someone needs to discuss something else.

Remind people that I am not a stereotype career woman – just an individual doing a job.

Keep a good sense of humour at all times.

In personnel, tendency to be regarded as 'dealing with secretaries' therefore deliberately involve oneself in higher level work, this means more pressure.

Work hard and play hard and know when the pressure is getting too great.

Type A coronary-prone behaviour pattern

As predicted by the authors in the earlier chapters, women in management have significantly higher average coronary-prone behaviour, Type A, scores as opossed to Type B (low risk of CHD) compared with men (see table 5.8).

TABLE 5.8   TYPE A CORONARY-PRONE BEHAVIOUR: SIGNIFICANT DIFFERENCES BETWEEN FEMALE AND MALE MANAGERS

Type A Score	Mean	SD	t	P
Females	81	11·3	−2·33	<0·020
Males	79	11.⁻		

The inventory we adopted yields scores ranging from 12 to 132, the higher scores being indicative of Type A behaviour. As well, these scores can be used roughly to designate an individual either as a Type A1 (score range 93–132), Type A2 (score range 80–92), Type B3 (score range 55-79), or Type B4 (score range 12–54). Type A1 signifies the most highly developed Type A behaviour and Type B4 the most extreme Type B behaviour (Bortner and Rosenman, 1967). Therefore, the mean score of 81 for female managers rests at the lower end of the Type A2 category, whilst the mean score of 79 for male managers is placed at the top end of the Type B3 category.

Furthermore, when the mean Type A scores are broken down by management levels, the highest score of 83·9 emerges for females in middle management which is significantly higher than the mean score of 78 for male middle managers. This would tend to support earlier studies (e.g. Waldron, *et al.* 1977; Waldron, 1978) which have suggested that working professional women usually show maximum Type A scores after the age of 30 years (i.e. predominantly middle management years), and gradually their scores decrease in their later years of working life.

Finally, it is interest to note that the lowest Type A scores for both sexes were from men and women *supervisors*. This is not a particularly unexpected finding, considering that several studies in the past have associated higher Type A scores with higher occupational status (Rosenman, *et al.* 1964; 1966).

One successful top female executive who was interviewed suggested how women should cope with their Type A behaviour:

(1) Being in touch with my anxiety and searching for the cause.
(2) Deliberately thinking of people in the situation.
(3) Talking about my anxieties.
(4) Trying to take a long-term perspective of success/failure.
(5) Trying to ensure people get to know me as a person so they can't stereotype me.
(6) Making notes, learning from experience what I would do in the same situation again.
(7) Allowing 'gestation' time during problem-solving, i.e. trying to let my subconscious work things out.
(8) Feeling confident about my appearance when in risk-taking situations.
(9) Acknowledging my successes to myself.
(10) Reading something away from the immediate 'problem' but around work to liken my mind and stimulate thinking.
(11) Aim to do one personal development/training activity a year – to take time to take stock, heighten awareness and get things into perspective.
(12) Keeping in touch with issues and problems outside work, e.g. family, politics, etc., to put mine into perspective.
(13) Looking for another door to push open when one has just shut.

Summary

We can conclude that women managers reported higher pressure levels stemming from stress factors at work, home and socially than did men managers. While managers of both sexes appear to use similar stress-coping strategies, women managers are more likely to have higher Type A scores. Finally, compared to male managers, female managers maintain they practise positive management styles more frequently.

CHAPTER 6

Problems faced by women and men at different rungs of the managerial ladder

An important part of our study concerned the isolation of problems and pressures experienced by managers at different rungs of the managerial ladder. Consequently, in this chapter we discuss the similarities and differences between the problems reported by women and men occupying junior, supervisory, middle and senior management.

Work stress factors

Table 6.1 isolates those causes of stress at work which scored higher pressure for female managers than male ones, differing significantly within management levels, but not overall. In particular, junior female managers appear to be more susceptible to specific work stress than their male counterparts. Office politics, for example, evolved as a high stress factor for junior women managers. This appears to confirm Harlan and Weiss's (1980) suggestion that more inexperienced female managers are often less effective at dealing with politics compared to their male counterparts, and that this is a combination of both inadequate training opportunities and socialization. Indeed, junior women in management reported significantly higher stress compared to junior male managers, with regard to 'inadequate job and training experience compared to colleagues of the opposite sex'.

Female junior managers also reported greater pressure from their 'poor work environment' and 'taking work home' in contrast to their junior male colleagues. Undoubtedly, the latter stressor may be linked with junior females feeling they have to do better at their jobs than their male counterparts.

TABLE 6.1   FEMALE STRESS FACTORS: SIGNIFICANT DIFFERENCES
WITHIN A PARTICULAR MANAGEMENT LEVEL

	Management level	Mean	SD	t	P
Taking work home					
Females	Junior	1·7	0·9	−2·11	<0·036
Males		1·3	0·7		
Office politics					
Females	Junior	2·6	1·3	−2·61	<0.010
Males		2·0	1·2		
Poor work environment					
Females	Junior	1·6	1·0	−2·31	<0·025
Males		1·3	0·7		
Working relationships with female superiors					
Females	Junior	1·4	0·9	−2.02	<0·047
Males		1·2	0·4		
Feeling isolated					
Females	Junior	1·7	1.0	−2.21	<0·031
Males		1·4	0·7		
Females	Senior	1·8	1·0	−2·08	<0·040
Males		1·5	0·8		
I feel uncomfortable working with members of the opposite sex					
Females	Middle	1·1	0.4	−2·39	<0.017
Males		1·0	0.2		

Concerning 'relationships at work', junior female managers reported significantly higher scores than men in
response to 'working relationships with female superiors'.
Couple this with the finding that more women managers
experience pressure due to prejudiced attitudes from the
members of the same sex at work (compared with male
managers: see table 5.4), one must not assume that 'relationship problems' for women are linked exclusively with men in
their work environment.

The token woman factor – 'feeling isolated' – is a cause of stress often associated with women managers being the minority sex in a male-dominated profession, and this was found to be significant for women both in junior and senior positions compared with men occupying similar management levels. In fact, feeling isolated was a high stress factor identified by junior managers in the qualitative part of the study as well (see table 3.8). Nevertheless, isolation is obviously not an exclusively female stress factor and feelings of isolation can have detrimental effects on men in positions of authority. This was found to be the case in our study, with regard to supervisory male managers.

Being a woman can also present a challenge in management, as one of our interviewees reflects:

As a woman who has made some headway in a male-dominated company, I think it has been of help to me to bear in mind the fact that I'm there to do a job irrespective of whether I'm male or female. I should expect no special treatment 'because I'm a woman', and no special acknowledgement/gratification from others. To work as a woman in our organization in a 'managerial' capacity does present some challenges, but it's nice to have challenges sometimes!

I do not believe, however, that adopting a women's libbist attitude would help – people do not react favourably to those who are there 'to make a point'. This comes back to my first point - I'm not ashamed/embarrassed/humiliated because I'm a woman – I'm quite happy about it and don't really feel it need influence the job that I'm there to do.

Women in middle management, on the other hand, reported significantly higher pressure scores than their male counterparts in response to the question, 'I feel uncomfortable working with members of the opposite sex', although both the mean scores were low.

Table 6.2 shows work factors in which higher mean work pressure scores existed for male managers than female ones, and which differed significantly within particular management levels, but not overall. Compared with their female counterparts, senior male managers reported greater pressures associated with 'lack of variety at work' and

TABLE 6.2 MALE STRESS FACTORS: SIGNIFICANT DIFFERENCES WITHIN A PARTICULAR MANAGEMENT LEVEL

	Management level	Mean	SD	t	P
Lack of variety at work					
Females	Senior	1·2	0·6	2·21	<0.030
Males		1·6	1·1		
Underpromotion – employed beneath my competence					
Females	Senior	1·9	1·3	2·86	<0.005
Males		2·6	1·4		
Playing the counsellor role at work					
Females	Junior	1·5	0·8	1·98	<0·049
Males		1·9	0·9		
Long working hours					
Females	Supervisory	1·7	1·1	2·71	<0.008
Males		2·5	1·1		

'underpromotion' – 'employed beneath my competence'. Moreover, 'underpromotion' was a particularly high stress factor for senior male managers.

In general, male managers are more dissatisfied with their pay than women managers, and even when they reach senior management, they appear to feel that they are still in positions below their competence. Junior male managers had significantly greater pressure scores related to 'playing the counsellor role at work' than females in junior management. This was a surprising finding; furthermore, male managers overall viewed this as a higher stress factor. Is it that men are having to play the counsellor role more at work compared to women, or that women find it easier to cope with that role?

The highest average pressure score in response to 'long working hours', came from male, as opposed to female, supervisors. While male supervisors were more likely to be working shifts than any other male or female managers at other levels, they did not view shift work itself as being a particularly high stress factor. Therefore, rather than shift work *per se* being a source of stress, perhaps the length of working hours per shift is a particular onerous pressure for male supervisors.

Home and social factors

With regard to the home and social factors in which significant differences between female and male managers were prevalent with a management level, but not overall, table 6.3 shows that male supervisors reported more pressure in connection with 'demands of work on my private/social life' than females in supervisory positions. Further, this is undoubtedly also linked with male supervisors' higher stress scores in connection with long working hours. Conversely, females in junior and middle management viewed the demands of work on their private/social life as a greater

TABLE 6.3   HOME AND SOCIAL FACTORS: SIGNIFICANT DIFFERENCES BETWEEN FEMALE AND MALE MANAGERS WITHIN A PARTICULAR MANAGEMENT LEVEL

	Management level	Mean	SD	t	P
Having to move with my job in order to progress in my career					
Females	Senior	2·4	1·4	−2·06	<0.042
Males		1·8	1·3		
Demands of work on my private/social life					
Females	Middle	2·1	1·3	−2·11	<0.036
Males		1·8	0·9		
Females	Junior	1·9	1·1	−2·71	<0·009
Males		1·5	0·7		
Females	Supervisory	1·4	0·8	−2·85	<0.005
Males		2·1	0·9		

source of stress than did their male counterparts. With the exception of supervisors, *women at all levels of the managerial hierarchy, in contrast to their male peers, believed the home and social factor to be a significant source of stress.*

The highest average pressure score for, 'having to move with my job in order to progress with my career', came from women in senior management, and was significantly greater than that for senior male managers. This is understandable if one relates back to the earlier qualitative data. Often, married women in senior management positions were not mobile because of their husbands' jobs, and those who were single (especially those living alone) did not want to sever the important support systems and social contacts they had built up in their community.

Some women believe that one should enter a career/marital contract with their spouses before entering management, as a woman manager indicated in our interview with her:

A demanding job can just as easily be tackled by a woman as by a man if a woman gets the same support at home as a man expects to get. Women should not enter into marriage without having agreed with their future spouse that he really will do 50 per cent of the housework, and that includes cooking! There also needs to be an agreement about mobility and an acceptance that *both* careers are important. This may involve agreeing not to move at all, which is fine if you live in a large conurbation but not so practical if you live in an area where there aren't promotion opportunities or your choice of profession demands movement.

Others feel it should be a career or a family, as this woman flight service manager says:

I have been in my present job for too long, because I am unwilling/unable to look for, or accept a promotion because it would mean a move in location. This I cannot do as I am married and it was agreed my husband's career came first. This naturally causes some frustrations both for me and my employer.

I have just become pregnant, at 38, so who knows the answer to the career woman's problem? I believe you cannot be married to a career conscious or successful spouse – you only need one in the family.

Others feel that they should pursue both a career in management and home, if they get support from their husbands, as this female advertising executive suggested:

Most of the pressure experienced personally comes from sharing myself between the demands of an over-busy working day and the demands of (i.e. support and homework help) three teenage children in the evenings/weekends. My husband is active in local politics as well as occupied with a full-time job; his support and help at evenings/weekends is consequently limited.

The following attitudes of mind, therefore, help me through:
(1) If I had the choice, I would continue working, not choose to spend my daytime at home.
(2) If I can survive for a few more years, the children's needs will have subsided.

I do, however, feel most strongly that advancement in management for married women with children is far harder than for married men with children. I feel that I need a wife! I would then have a chance to make of my job what I would wish.

Positive coping strategies

When reviewing the frequency with which the female and male samples used relaxation techniques such as meditation and yoga or strategies such as leaving their work area and going somewhere in order to relax, neither technique was particularly popular. However, it was found that junior male managers were significantly less likely to use relaxation methods such as meditation than were junior female managers, whereas female supervisors left their work area less frequently, in order to relax, than did their male counterparts.

Management style

There were two differences between female and male managers in relation to the frequency with which they adopted different management styles. These were significant within management level but not overall. Women in middle management maintained they more often adopted an *authoritative* and *positive* style than middle-management males. Once again, this finding is in conflict with the popular myth that women have problems asserting the authoritative aspects of their leadership. Indeed, in general, male managers seem to find this aspect of the job more of a source of stress than females (e.g. managing people, disciplining subordinates, being 'the boss').

The important point is surely for women managers to examine their management style carefully, as a senior executive in the retail trade indicated to us:

One of the most important things I've found in coping with pressures of being a woman in 'management' has been to have a group of women in similar positions which I could turn to for support and confirmation. I've also found it important to 'think through' carefully my non-authoritarian style and to be clear that this is a valid and important way of operating, particularly in educational management. It's often implied that this is weak or disorganized and male-dominated organizations tend to undermine this style, so I've found an understanding and analysis of this to be important.

Sources of stress for female and male managers overall and within management levels

The final stage of the analysis of stress at work involved the isolation and comparison of high stress factors for female and male managers overall and within management levels. It was decided that a high stress factor constituted a mean pressure score of 2·5 or above (1=no pressure at all to 5=a great deal of pressure) in response to questions dealing with job, organizational, home and social factors.

High stress factors in senior management

For both females and males in senior management positions, 'work overload' and 'time pressures/deadlines' were viewed as high stress factors. Unlike senior women managers, however, males in senior positions also found 'underpromotion – being employed beneath their competence', a significantly high stress factor. 'Thwarted ambition' and 'dissatisfaction with the degree to which there is job advancement' has been found to be a cause of stress for male managers in the past (Marshall and Cooper, 1979). Nonetheless, it is interesting that this is a high stress factor only for males in the higher levels of the management hierarchy. One could

TABLE 6.4   HIGH STRESS FACTORS FOR FEMALE MANAGERS OVERALL AND WITHIN MANAGEMENT LEVELS

Management level	Source of stress	Mean	SD
Senior	Work overload	2·9	1·1
	Time pressures/deadlines	2·7	1·2
	Lack of consultation/communication	2·5	1·2
Middle	Work overload	2·8	1·1
	Time pressures/deadlines	2·9	1·2
	Feeling I have to perform better at my job than colleagues of the opposite sex	2·5**	1·4
	Lack of consultation/communication	2·8	1·3
	My career-related dilemma concerning whether to start a family	2·6**	1·6
Junior	Work overload	2·7	1·1
	Time pressures/deadlines	2·8	1·1
	Feeling undervalued	2·5	1·3
	I feel my sex is a disadvantage when it comes to job promotion/career progress prospects	2·5**	1·4
	Unclear career prospects	2·6	1·3
	Office politics	2·6*	1·3
	My career-related dilemma concerning whether to start a family	2·6*	1·5
Supervisory	Time pressures/deadlines	2·7	1·2
	Lack of consultation/communication	2·7	1·3
Total sample	Work overload	2·6	1·1
	Time pressures/deadlines	2·8	1·2
	Lack of consultation/communication	2·7	1·3
	My career-related dilemma concerning whether to start a family	2·5**	1·5

  * $P<0·01$
** $P<0·001$

TABLE 6.5 HIGH STRESS FACTORS FOR MALE MANAGERS:
OVERALL AND WITHIN MANAGEMENT LEVELS

Management level	Source of stress	Mean	SD
Senior	Work overload	3·0	1·1
	Time pressures/deadlines	3·0	1·1
	Underpromotion	2·6**	1·2
Middle	Work overload	2·7	1·0
	Time pressures/deadlines	2·9	1·0
	Sacking someone	2·5	1·4
	Rate of pay	2·6*	1·1
	Lack of consultation/communication	2·6	1·2
Junior	Work overload	2·6	1·1
	Time pressures/deadlines	2·8	1·1
	Disciplining subordinates	2·5**	1·1
	Sacking someone	2·7	1·7
	Underpromotion	2·6	1·2
Supervisory	Work overload	2·7	1·2
	Time pressures/deadlines	2·9	1·1
	Long working hours	2·5**	1·1
	Staff shortages and staff turnover rates	2·5	1·2
	Equipment failures	2·9	1·2
	Unclear career prospects	2·6	1·3
	Rate of pay	2·5	1·1
	Lack of consultation/communication	2·9	1·3
	Redundancy threat	2·6	1·3
Total sample	Work overload	2·7	1·1
	Time pressures/deadlines	2·9	1·1
	Underpromotion	2·5	1·3
	Lack of consultation/communication	2·5	1·2

* $P<0.05$
** $P<0.01$

assume they are a highly ambitious group who feel they
should be in positions 'above their station'. The other high
stress factor for senior women managers, not shared with
their male counterparts, was 'lack of consultation/com-
munication'. Moreover, this could possibly be due to the fact
that there are fewer women in senior management than in

any of the other managerial levels and they report the highest pressure in connection with 'feeling isolated', along with middle management women.

High stress factors in middle management

Both women and men in middle management reported five high stress factors, three of which were common to both groups (i.e. 'work overload', 'time pressures/deadlines', and 'lack of consultation/communication') (see tables 6.4 and 6.5). On the other hand, women middle managers found performance pressure ('feeling I have to perform better at my job than colleagues of the opposite sex') a significantly higher stress factor than their male counterparts. This was also the case in relation to the other high stress factors for women concerning 'my career-related dilemma concerning whether to start a family'. Middle-management males, however, rated 'sacking someone' as a high stress factor along with 'rate of pay'. In fact, rate of pay was a significantly higher stress factor for middle-management males, even though they tended to earn more than their female middle-manager colleagues.

High stress factors in junior management

Compared with women in all the other management levels, those in junior management reported the most number of high stress factors (i.e. a total of seven). Both men and women in junior management shared the high stress factors associated with 'work overload' and 'time pressures/deadlines'.

In terms of career development factors, female junior managers unfortunately believed that their sex 'is a disadvantage when it comes to job promotion/career progress prospects'. This was a significantly higher stress factor for them than for junior male managers. In addition, junior female managers identified 'unclear career prospects' as being a source of tension for them. But, like senior management men, junior male managers reported their major stress factor as being 'underpromotion – employed beneath my competence'.

The two other high stress factors which were significantly greater for junior female managers than their male counterparts, were 'office politics' and 'my career-related dilemma concerning whether to start a family'. This child-bearing dilemma was also a high stress factor for women in middle management. Interestingly, junior male managers report more pressure associated with the authoritative aspects of management (i.e. 'sacking someone' and 'disciplining subordinates'). In fact, men in middle management also highlighted having to 'sack someone' as being a particular pressure point for them.

High stress factors for supervisors

Female supervisors only reported two major stress factors: 'time pressures/deadlines' and 'lack of consultation/communication', both of which they shared with male supervisors. But, in comparison with males in all the other levels of the managerial hierarchy, male supervisors reported the greatest number of stress factors (i.e. nine in total). Along with male middle managers, male supervisors felt that their rate of pay caused them high pressure. They viewed their long working hours as a significantly higher stress factor compared with female supervisors, and also saw work overload as being a source of tension.

When it came to career development, male supervisors reported 'unclear career prospects' as being a source of stress and were the only management level in both female and male samples, who classed 'redundancy threat' as a significant source of personal concern. This is probably due to the fact that the less qualified are more susceptible to redundancies and males in supervisory positions *may* see their role as a wage earner as being more vital than female supervisors. Alternatively, perhaps the threat of unemployment is more of a worry to men than it is to women.

The two other sources of high stress for male supervisors related to 'staff shortages' and 'staff turnover rates', along with 'equipment failures'. When interviewing women supervisors, the author discovered that male supervisors are often expected to also repair and maintain their subordinate's equipment and machinery (this tends not to be the case for female supervisors). Consequently, it is not surprising that equipment failures are seen as a high stress factor for male supervisors.

High stress factors for all female and male managers

When examining the overall high stress factors for the total sample of the women and men at all levels of the management hierarchy, they share the following three: 'work overload', 'time pressures/deadlines' and 'lack of consultation/communication'. Nevertheless, a significantly higher stress factor unique to female managers was their 'career-related dilemma concerning whether to start a family'. Obviously, the conflict over whether or not to have a child is a very real source of stress for the career-orientated woman manager.

Conversely, male managers overall, isolated 'underpromotion – employed beneath my competence' as a high stress factor. In contrast, underpromotion was not highlighted as a source of stress by women at any level of management. As in the case of rate of pay, this indicates that women managers appear to be more satisfied with their situation in terms of present job level compared with their male counterparts.

CHAPTER 7

The cost of stress

Having reviewed the reported sources of stress of managers of both sexes, we now turn our attention to the cost of that stress in terms of health and behaviour. The five major health behaviour factors we examined in Phase 2 of this study were: general health symptom list, cigarette smoking, alcohol consumption, job satisfaction, and work performance factors. No significant differences were found between female and male managers overall or within different management levels in relation to any aspect of their cigarette smoking habits or degrees of job satisfaction. Differences were found, however, in their general health, alcohol consumption and work performance.

General health

Of the 20 symptoms itemized in the modified version of the Gurin Psychosomatic Symptom List (Gurin, *et al.*, 1960), female managers had significantly higher scores on general health symptoms. An examination of the data presented in table 7.1 reveals that the only symptom for which male managers gave a significantly higher average score was associated with 'being bothered by having an upset stomach'. Stress-related stomach ailments such as ulcers are still more common in men than women (Selye, 1976; Wingerson, 1981).

The symptom ranked as most common by women managers was 'tiredness' – a finding which replicates the authors' earlier interview results. Predictably, this was followed by 'finding it difficult to get up in the morning', and then by the

TABLE 7.1   GENERAL HEALTH QUESTIONNAIRE: SIGNIFICANT
DIFFERENCES BETWEEN FEMALE AND MALE MANAGERS

	Mean	SD	t	P
Have you ever been bothered by nervousness, feeling fidgety or tense?				
Females	2·6	0·9	−3·41	<0·001
Males	2·4	0·9		
Are you ever troubled by headaches or pains in the head?				
Females	2·4	0·9	−4·9	<0.001
Males	2·0	0·9		
Are there any times when you just don't feel like eating?				
Females	1·9	0·9	−2·73	<0.006
Males	1·7	0·8		
Are there times when you get tired very easily?				
Females	3·0	0·9	−7·54	<0·001
Males	2·4	0·9		
How often are you bothered by having an upset stomach?				
Females	1·9	0·9	2·8	<0·005
Males	2·0	0·9		
Do you find it difficult to get up in the morning?				
Females	2·7	1·2	−4·05	<0·001
Males	2·3	1·1		
Are there times when you tend to cry easily?				
Females	2·2	0·8	−21·42	<0·001
Males	1·2	0·4		
Do you ever have spells of dizziness?				
Females	1·5	0·7	−3·86	<0·001
Males	1·3	0·5		

TABLE 7.1   *(continued)*

	Mean	SD	t	P
Are you ever bothered by nightmares?				
Females	1·5	0·7	−5·08	<0.001
Males	1·3	0·5		
Do you ever feel mentally exhausted and have difficulty in concentrating or thinking clearly?				
Females	2·3	0·8	−2·43	<0·015
Males	2·2	0·8		
Do you ever want to be left alone?				
Females	2·6	0·8	−3·44	<0·001
Males	2·3	0·8		
Total health score				
Females	47·1	11·0	−4·37	<0·001
Males	43·6	9·6		

desire 'to want to be left alone' and 'being bothered by nervousness, feeling fidgety or tense'.

Significantly higher average scores were reported by women in contrast to men managers in response to 'being troubled by headaches or pains in the head'. Moreover, recent research (Wilkinson, 1980) has shown that migraines and headaches affect three times as many working women as working men. Over a quarter of the authors' sample of senior female executives listed in *Who's Who?* complained of suffering from migraine (Davidson and Cooper, 1980a).

'Mental exhaustion and having difficulty in concentrating or thinking clearly', followed by tending 'to cry easily', were experienced more frequently by women managers than their male counterparts. The other symptoms over which women had significantly higher scores were 'not feeling like eating', 'having spells of dizziness' and 'being bothered by nightmares'.

When examining the overall health scores of the female and male managers, not surprisingly, females are much more at risk. As the emphasis was on the current physical state and all respondents were requested to report their frequency of symptoms for the previous three months only, one can conclude that, overall, women reported poorer health compared with men managers. Nevertheless, there are two important issues which need to be emphasized. Firstly, the female sample were a slighly older population than the male sample, and health tends to worsen with age (Seyle, 1976). Secondly, the potential range of total health scores was from 25, indicating extremely good health, to 107, indicating extremely poor health. Neither the female nor male managers' scores were particularly high, and both were in the middle range between good and poor health.

Drug use and alcoholism

In order to determine the frequency with which the female and male samples took drugs in order to help them relax, respondents were asked how often (1=never to 5=always) they took aspirin; used tranquillizers or other medication; drank coffee or Coke or ate frequently; smoked or had an alcoholic drink (Steinmetz, 1979). The only significant difference was that male managers were more likely to have an alcoholic drink than female managers (see table 7.2).

TABLE 7.2   DRUG USE: SIGNIFICANT DIFFERENCES BETWEEN FEMALE AND MALE MANAGERS

	Mean	SD	t	P
Have an alcoholic drink?				
Females	2·6	1·0	2·38	<0·018
Males	2·8	1·1		
Alcohol drinking habits (1 = teetotal to 6 = more than 6 drinks a day)				
Females	2·7	8·8	3·91	<0.000
Males	3·0	1·1		

In fact, with the exception of male and female supervisors, having an alcoholic drink was the most popular method of coping with stress for men and women at all levels of management. Drinking coffee or Coke or eating frequently was the next most common method of relaxation adopted by both female and male managers, followed by smoking, taking aspirin and using tranquillizers or other medication. The alcohol-drinking habits of both samples were examined in more detail and it was seen that male managers drank significantly more alcohol than female ones (see table 7.2). For women managers, alcohol consumption increased with management level and the heaviest drinkers were women in senior management. However, males in middle management drank the most alcohol, followed by senior, junior and supervisory managers, in that order. Of the total female management group, 4·2 per cent were teetotal, compared to 2·7 per cent of male managers, 12·1 per cent of women as opposed to 13 per cent of men drank regularly one or two drinks a day, and only 2·6 per cent of women managers drank regularly three to six drinks a day, compared to 10·8 per cent of men managers. No female manager reported drinking regularly more than six drinks a day in contrast to 1·6 per cent of her male counterparts.

Work performance

In order to measure work performance, 16 measures were included and respondents were asked how often they felt the following to be a source of stress at work (using the 5-point Likert scale from 1 (never) to 5 (always)). From the data presented in table 7.3 it can be seen that on only one work performance factor – 'unable to produce a satisfactory quantity of work' – did male managers report a significantly higher score than women managers.

Conversely, women managers reported significantly higher detrimental work performance scores on six behaviour items: 'being unable to "sell themselves" in competitive situations (inadequate self presentation)'; 'being unable to cope well in conflict situations'; 'lacking self-confidence in their ability to do their job'; 'lacking confidence

TABLE 7.3   WORK PERFORMANCE: SIGNIFICANT DIFFERENCES
BETWEEN FEMALE AND MALE MANAGERS

How often do you feel the following at work?	Mean	SD	t	P
Unable to produce a satisfactory quantity of work?				
Females	1·9	0·8	2·12	<0·034
Males	2·0	0·8		
Lack confidence in putting forward my point of view (e.g. at meetings)				
Females	2·2	1·0	−3·55	<0·001
Males	1·9	0·9		
Unable to be successful				
Females	2·2	0·9	−3·81	<0·001
Males	1·9	0·8		
Unable to 'sell myself' in competitive situations (inadequate self presentation)				
Females	2·5	0·1	−2·54	<0·011
Males	2·3	0·8		
Unable to cope well in conflict situations				
Females	2·4	0·9	−3·95	<0·001
Males	2·2	0·7		
Reacting too emotionally when faced with problems at work				
Females	2·2	0·9	−3·83	<0·001
Males	2·0	0·8		
Lack of self-confidence in the ability to do my job				
Females	1·9	0·9	−4.97	<0·001
Males	1·6	0·7		

in putting forward their point of view '(e.g. at meetings'); 'reacting too emotionally when faced with problems at work'; and 'being unable to be successful'. Hence, overall, women in management appear to suffer more frequently in terms of satisfactory work performance. This particularly seems to be the case in relation to behaviour assciated with confidence and assertion.

Differences between male and female managers at various levels of the managerial hierarchy

General health

There were three health measures whereby differences between the female and male samples were significant within a particular management level, but not overall, and they were all items listed in the General Health Questionnaire. Table 7.4 illustrates that 'trouble getting to sleep or staying asleep' was a significantly higher outcome of stress for

TABLE 7.4   GENERAL HEALTH QUESTIONNAIRE: SIGNIFICANT DIFFERENCES BETWEEN FEMALE AND MALE MANAGERS WITHIN PARTICULAR MANAGEMENT LEVELS

	Manage-ment level	Mean	SD	t	P
Do you ever have trouble getting to sleep or staying asleep?					
Females	Middle	2·5	1·0	−2·10	<0·037
Males		2·2	1·0		
Does ill-health ever affect the amount of work you do?					
Females	Junior	1·8	0·8	−2·81	<0.007
Males		1·5	0·6		
Do your muscles ever tremble enough to bother you (e.g. hands tremble, eyes twitch)?					
Females	Junior	1·4	0·7	−2·78	<0.007
Males		1·2	0·5		

middle-management women in contrast to middle-management men. On the other hand, women in junior management compared to their male counterparts were significantly more susceptible to their 'muscles ever trembling enough to bother them' and by 'ill-health ever affecting the amount of work they do'.

High stress outcomes

The last section of the analysis of the dependent variable results consists of the isolation and comparison of high stress outcomes for female and male managers within management levels and overall. It was thought that a high stress outcome would constitute a fairly high mean score (2·5 or more) in response to questions listed in the General Health Questionnaire; job satisfaction, the use of drugs in order to relax, and work performance measures. In relation to alcohol and cigarette consumption, these were viewed as high stress-related behaviours if the consumption rates exceeded those found by previous researchers using comparable populations. Table 7.5 shows the high stress outcomes for female

TABLE 7.5   HIGH STRESS OUTCOMES FOR FEMALE MANAGERS: OVERALL AND WITHIN MANAGEMENT LEVEL

	Mean	SD
Senior		
Bothered by nervousness, feeling fidgety or tense	2·7	0·9
Get tired very easily	2·9*	0·9
Difficult to get up in the morning	2·7*	1·2
Smoke, drink or eat more than you should	2·8	1·0
Just want to be left alone	2·6	0·8
Drink coffee, Coke or eat frequently in order to relax	2·7	1·1
Have alcoholic drink in order to relax	2·8	0·1
Smoking cigarettes		
Middle		
Trouble getting to sleep or staying asleep	2·5*	1·0
Bothered by nervousness, feeling fidgety or tense	2·7*	0·9
Get tired very easily	3·1***	0·9
Difficult to get up in the morning	2·7*	1·2
Smoke, drink or eat more than you should	2·8	1·1
Just want to be left alone	2·5	0·9

TABLE 7.5   *(continued)*

	Mean	SD
Drink coffee, Coke or eat frequently in order to relax	2·6	1·2
Have alcoholic drink in order to relax	2·7	1·0
Unable to influence and persuade people	2·5	0·8
Unable to 'sell myself' in competitive situations	2·5	1·0
Unable to cope well in conflict situations	2·5***	0·9
Making mistakes	2·6	0·6
Smoking cigarettes		

Junior

	Mean	SD
Bothered by nervousness, feeling. fidgety or tense	2·7***	0·9
Get tired very easily	3·0***	0·9
Difficult to get up in the morning	2·8*	1·2
Smoke, drink or eat more than you should	2·7	1·0
Just want to be left alone	2·6*	0·8
Drink coffee, Coke or eat frequently in order to relax	2·7	1·1
Have alcoholic drink in order to relax	2·6	0·9
Unable to use my skills and knowledge	2·5	1·0
Unable to 'sell myself' in competitive situations	2·6	1·0
Unable to cope well in conflict situations	2·5*	0·8
Making mistakes	2·5	0·5

Supervisory

	Mean	SD
Bothered by nervousness, feeling fidgety or tense	2·5	0·9
Troubled by headaches and pains in the head	2·5	1·0
Get tired very easily	2·9	0·9
Difficult to get up in the morning	2·5	1·2
Smoke, drink or eat more than you should	2·6	1·1
Just want to be left alone	2·6	0·9
Drink coffee, Coke or eat frequently in order to relax	2·5	1·2
Making mistakes	2·5	0·7

Total sample

	Mean	SD
Bothered by nervousness, feeling fidgety or tense	2·6***	0·9
Get tired very easily	3·0***	0·9
Difficult to get up in the morning	2·7***	1·2
Smoke, drink or eat more than you should	2·7	0·7
Just want to be left alone	2·6***	0·8
Drink coffee, Coke or eat frequently in order to relax	2·6	1·5
Have alcoholic drink in order to relax	2·6	1·0
Unable to 'sell myself' in competitive situations	2·5*	1·0
Making mistakes	2·5	0·6

* $P<0.05$ ** $P<0.01$ *** $P<0.001$

managers overall, and within management levels. Table 7.6 reveals the high stress outcomes for male managers overall, and within management levels.

TABLE 7.6   HIGH STRESS OUTCOMES FOR MALE MANAGERS: OVERALL AND WITHIN MANAGEMENT LEVEL

	Mean	SD
Senior		
Bothered by nervousness, feeling fidgety or tense	2·6	0·9
Get tired very easily	2·5	0·9
Smoke, drink or eat more than you should	2·9	1·0
Drink coffee, Coke or eat frequently in order to relax	2·7	1·1
Have alcoholic drink in order to relax	2·8	1·1
Making mistakes	2·5	0·6
Middle		
Smoke, drink or eat more than you should	2·7	0·9
Drink coffee, Coke or eat frequently in order to relax	2·6	1·2
Have alcoholic drink in order to relax	2·8	1·1
Unable to use my skills and knowledge	2·5	0·9
Making mistakes	2·5	0·6
Junior		
Smoke, drink or eat more than you should	2·5	1·0
Drink coffee, Coke or eat frequently in order to relax	2·7	1·1
Have alcoholic drink in order to relax	2·8	1·0
Unable to use my skills and knowledge	2·5	1·0
Unable to influence and persuade people	2·5	0·7
Unable to 'sell myself' in competitive situations	2·5	0·8
Supervisory		
Trouble getting to sleep or staying asleep	2·5	0·8
Get tired very easily	2·6	0·7
Difficult to get up in the morning	2·6	1·3
Smoke, drink or eat more than you should	2·6	1·0
Just want to be left alone	2·5	0·9
Drink coffee, Coke or eat frequently in order to relax	2·5	1·2
I do not find real enjoyment in my work (job dissatisfaction)	2·5	1·4
Total sample		
Smoke, drink or eat more than you should	2·7	1·0
Drink coffee, Coke or eat frequently in order to relax	2·6	1·5
Have alcoholic drink in order to relax	2·8*	1·1

* $P < 0.05$

SENIOR MANAGEMENT

Women and men in senior management share three high stress general health symptoms 'being bothered by nervousness, feeling fidgety or tense'; 'getting tired very easily'; and 'smoking, drinking or eating more than they should'. Senior female managers reported a further two high stress health symptoms concerning 'difficulty in getting up in the morning' and 'wanting to be left alone'.

Two common high stress outcomes related to drug use for relaxation for both senior female and male managers were 'drinking coffee, Coke or eating frequently' and 'having an alcoholic drink'. While male managers at all levels tended to drink more alcohol than their female counterparts, their alcohol consumption rate tended not to exceed those found by Cooper and Melhuish (1980) in their study of 500 senior male managers.

Nevertheless, this was not the case when examining the senior female managers' cigarette smoking behaviour. In spite of more male managers in the authors' study having given up smoking compared with women managers (i.e. 25·1 per cent and 17·3 per cent respectively), a higher percentage of women managers (32·4 per cent) were smokers compared to male managers (31·1 per cent). According to a survey by Wingerson (1981) in 1980, 21 per cent of professional women aged 16 and over smoked, 33 per cent of female employers/managers, and 34 per cent of women occupying intermediate and junior non-manual positions (see table 2.2). However, 39·4 per cent of senior female managers in the authors' sample smoked, compared to 37·7 per cent of senior male managers, which is a higher proportion of smokers than those found in Wingerson's (1981) categories of either professional women or women employers/managers. Moreover, women in senior management were more likely to smoke and to smoke more cigarettes a day, compared to both males and females at other management levels.

Senior female managers reported no high stress outcomes associated with work performance, but males in senior positions highlighted 'making mistakes' as a significant detrimental work performance variable.

MIDDLE MANAGEMENT

Women holding middle management positions had the greatest number of high stress outcome variables, a number far in excess of those reported by middle management male respondents. Both female and male middle managers shared the high stress general health symptom of 'smoking, drinking or eating more than they should'. In addition, women middle managers were often bothered by 'nervousness, feeling fidgety or tense'; 'getting tired very easily'; 'finding it difficult to get up in the morning'; and 'wanting to be left alone' – high stress health symptoms they also shared in common with senior female managers. Middle management women also complained of often 'having trouble in getting to sleep or staying asleep'.

Like their senior management counterparts, both female and male middle managers adopted the same two drug taking habits in order to relax, i.e. 'drinking coffee, Coke or eating frequently' and 'having an alcoholic drink'. In fact middle management males drank more alcohol than either men or women in any of the other management levels, but overall their alcohol consumption rate did not exceed that of the senior male executives in Cooper and Melhuish's (1980) study.

'Making mistakes' was the only detrimental work performance factor reported by both female and males at middle management level. The other performance item highlighted by male middle managers was to do with being 'unable to use their skills and knowledge'. Middle management women, on the other hand, frequently maintained they were 'unable to influence and persuade people', 'unable to "sell themselves" in competitive situations', and 'unable to cope well in conflict situations'.

Finally, in comparison with professional women and women employers/managers in Britain (Wingerson, 1981), a higher percentage of middle management women (i.e. 35·1 per cent) smoked cigarettes. A lower figure of 31·9 per cent of middle management men were smokers at the time of the survey.

JUNIOR MANAGEMENT

Junior females and male managers maintained they frequently 'smoked, drank or ate more than they should'. As with women in all the other management levels, junior women managers reported more high stress outcomes in relation to ill-health symptoms than did their male counterparts. Like the women holding senior and middle management jobs, junior women managers were frequently bothered by 'nervousness, feeling fidgety or tense', 'getting tired very easily', 'finding it difficult to get up in the morning', and often 'wanting to be left alone'.

As with senior and middle managers of both sexes, junior female and male managers frequently 'drank coffee, Coke or ate frequently' in order to relax, as well as 'having an alcoholic drink'. Both female and male junior managers believed they were frequently 'unable to use their skills and knowledge' at work and were 'unable to "sell themselves" in competitive situations'. However, junior male managers maintained they were frequently 'unable to influence and persuade people', whereas women in junior management in accordance with middle management women, reported often being 'unable to cope well in conflict situations' and 'making mistakes' at work.

SUPERVISORS

Female and male supervisors both frequently reported ill-health symptoms: 'getting tired very easily'; 'difficulty in getting up in the morning'; 'smoking, drinking or eating more than they should'; and 'just wanting to be left alone'.

Male supervisors also 'drank coffee, Coke or ate' in order to relax, but unlike the other male and female managers, they did not frequently resort to having an alcoholic drink. The only detrimental work performance factor which emerged for male and female supervisors, was the high frequency of 'making mistakes' on behalf of women supervisors. Nevertheless, what was interesting was the finding that male supervisors were the only management category of either sex, to give a high job dissatisfaction score in response to the statement, 'I find real enjoyment in my work'. The mean job satisfaction scores for the total female and male managers' sample to the two items, 'I feel fairly well satisfied with my present job' and 'I find real enjoyment in my work', was 2·2 and 2·1 respectively (on a 1 to 5 agree to disagree scale). Certainly, job satisfaction on the part of male supervisors is probably linked to the finding that they reported a greater number of high stress factors than any of the other male or female management categories (see tables 6.4 and 6.5).

SUMMARY OF HIGH STRESS OUTCOMES

Analysing the overall high stress outcomes for the total sample of female and male managers, it can be seen that a greater number were identified by the female sample. Five high stress health symptoms were often reported by women managers and four of these were experienced significantly more frequently by the women compared with the men, i.e. 'being bothered by nervousness, feeling fidgety or tense', 'getting tired very easily', 'finding it difficult to get up in the morning' and just 'wanting to be left alone'.

Both female and male managers claimed they frequently 'smoked, drank or ate more than they should', 'drank coffee, Coke or ate frequently in order to relax' and had an 'alcoholic drink' as a method of relaxation – the male managers doing this significantly more often than the females. Unlike the total female managerial sample, there were no detrimental work performance factors emerging for the total male sample. Conversely, overall, women managers felt they were frequently 'unable to "sell themselves" in competitive situations' and often 'made mistakes'. Clearly, these are work performance issues which have important implications in relation to management training and will be discussed in the final chapter.

CHAPTER 8

Stress vulnerability profiles

The results presented up to this point have described the major differences between female and male managers in relation to various sources of stress and health manifestations. The final major analysis of the data aims to identify any relationship between each of the five health variables: total general health score, cigarette consumption, alcohol consumption, job satisfaction and work performance – and the variety of potential sources of work stress. In order to identify and compare the predictors of each of the health measures for the female and male populations, the multivariate statistical techniques of step-wise multiple regression analysis was used independently on the total female manager sample and the total male manager sample. This is a method of achieving the best linear prediction equation between a given set of independent variables and the dependent variable in question. However, before the analysis could be carried out, it was necessary to reduce the large number of stress factor variables using the method of factor analysis.

Sources of work stress

Factor analysis is a technique which has been widely used in the social sciences and is a multivariate analytical technique for determining the interdependencies of variables, expressed as underlying dimensions or factors (Child, 1970). The factor analysis was carried out on the 79 independent stressor variables: job, organizational, home and social characteristics (independently for both female and male managers).

TABLE 8.1   WORK STRESS VARIABLES WHICH GROUP TOGETHER
FOR FEMALE MANAGERS

Factor 1   (54.7 per cent): 'The organization'
Lack of support from superiors   0·66
Lack of consultation and communication   0·64
Lack of encouragement from superiors   0·63
Lack of power and influence   0·60
Clarity of my job role/job duties   0·54
Underpromotion – employed beneath my competence   0·52
Inadequate feedback on my work   0·52
My beliefs conflicting with those of the company/organization   0·49
Feeling undervalued   0·46
Unclear career progress prospects   0·45
Inadequate supervision   0·44
Office politics   0·42
Lack of control in my work environment   0·54

Factor 2   (14·4 per cent): 'Leadership/Authority role'
Managing/supervising people   0·69
Disciplining subordinates   0·66
Being 'the boss'   0·62
Working relationships with female subordinates   0·51
Working relationships with female colleagues/peers   0·46
Working relationships with male subordinates   0·43
Playing the counsellor role at work   0·41

Factor 3   (9·2 per cent): 'Home/Partner relationships'
Demands of work on my relationship with spouse/partner   0·77
My spouse/partner's attitude towards my career   0·69
Conflicting responsibilities associated with running a
   home and career   0·61
Lack of domestic support at home   0·52
Lack of emotional support at home   0·49
Earning more than my spouse/partner   0·43

In the female manager sample, six factors were found
(table 8.1), while in the male manager sample eight factors
were discovered (table 8·2).

Individual factors and stress

The other stress factors to be included in multiple regression
analysis were already in a suitable format. They constituted:
appropriate indices of personal and job demographics, posi-

TABLE 8.1   (*continued*)

Factor 4   (8·5 per cent): 'Sex discrimination'
Sex discrimination and prejudice   0·77
Experiencing prejudiced attitudes from members of the
   opposite sex at work because of my sex   0·77
Colleagues of the opposite sex being treated more favourably
   by management   0·64
I feel my sex is a disadvantage when it comes to job
   promotion/career progress prospects   0·63
Members of the opposite sex at work try and force me into
   behaviours they associate with my sex, rather than letting me
   'be myself'   0·56
Feeling I have to perform better at my job than colleagues of the
   opposite sex   0·53
Inadequate job and training experience compared to colleagues
   of the opposite sex   0·46
Working relationships with male colleagues/peers   0·46
Working relationships with male superiors   0·42

Factor 5   (7·5 per cent): 'Work load'
Work overload   0·69
Long working hours   0·60
Taking my work home   0·58
Time pressures and deadlines   0·53
Demands of work on my private/social life   0·48
Administration and paperwork   0·48
Work underload   0·41

Factor 6   (5·7 per cent): 'Being single'
Being single I am sometimes excluded from social and business
   events such as dinner parties   0·63
Being single, other people sometimes label me as a bit of an
   'oddity'   0·63

---

tive coping strategies, management styles, and coronary-prone Type A behaviour. These are described briefly below.

Personal and job demographics
The personal and job demographics in the analysis included: age, marital status; number of children; educational attainment; management level; total number of years of full-time employment in life-time; the total number of companies/organizations worked for; annual salary; number

TABLE 8.2   WORK STRESS VARIABLES WHICH GROUP TOGETHER
FOR MALE MANAGERS

Factor 1   (35·4 per cent): 'Leadership/authority role'

Being 'the boss'	0·65
Disciplining subordinates	0·64
Managing/supervising people	0·54
New challenges and risk	0·50
Working relationships with male subordinates	0·44
Playing the counsellor role at work	0·43
Sacking someone	0·42
Inadequate supervision	0·42

Factor 2   (13·4 per cent): 'The organization'

Lack of consultation and communication	0·73
Clarity of my job role/job duties	0·67
My beliefs conflicting with those of the company	0·58
Lack of power and influence	0·58
Lack of control in my work environment	0·57
Lack of support from superiors	0·55
Lack of encouragement from superiors	0·50
Office politics	0·42
Feeling undervalued	0·40

Factor 3   (9·2 per cent): 'Work load'

Taking my work home	0·72
Long working hours	0·53
Work overload	0·50
Demands of work on my relationship with my children	0·48
Administration and paperwork	0·47
Demands of work on my relationship with spouse/partner	0·44
Time pressures and deadlines	0·43
The amount of travel required by my work	0·42

Factor 4   (8·2 per cent): 'Being single'

Being single, other people sometimes label me as a bit of an 'oddity'	0·78
Being single I am sometimes excluded from social and business events such as dinner parties	0·71
Lack of same sex role models – person of the same sex in a position above me, acting as an example	0·59
Feeling I have to perform better at my job than colleagues of the opposite sex	0·50
Lack of domestic support at home	0·49

TABLE 8.2   (*continued*)

Factor 5   (7 per cent): 'Alienation'
Sexual harassment of a verbal or physical nature	0·51
Business travel and staying in hotels alone	0·49
Overpromotion – promoted beyond my competence	0·47
Experiencing prejudiced attitudes from members of the same sex at work because of my sex	0·42

Factor 6   (6·3 per cent): 'Prejudice'
Members of the opposite sex at work try and force me into behaviours they associate with my sex, rather than letting me 'be myself'	0·75
Experiencing prejudiced attitudes from members of the opposite sex at work because of my sex	0·68

Factor 7   (5·7 per cent): 'Home/Partner relationships'
My spouse/partner's attitude towards my career	0·59
Lack of emotional support at home	0·53
Earning more than my spouse/partner	0·53
Conflicting responsibilities associated with running a home and career	0·52
Demands of work on my relationship with spouse/partner	0·49
Lack of domestic support at home	0·48

Factor 8   (5·3 per cent): 'Relationships at work'
Working relationships with female colleagues/peers	0·64
Working relationships with female subordinates	0·62
Working relationships with male subordinates	0·50
Members of the opposite sex seem uncomfortable working with me because of my sex	0·45
I feel uncomfortable working with members of the opposite sex	0·41

---

of persons supervised; the total number of employees in company/organization; and company gender constitution.

Positive coping strategies
The positive coping strategies included the indices measuring the frequency with which respondents adopted the following strategies to relax: relaxation techniques (meditation, yoga); informal relaxation techniques (i.e. take time out for

deep breathing, imagining pleasant scenes); exercise; talk to someone you know; leave the work area and go somewhere (time out, sick days, lunch away from organization, etc.); and use of humour.

Management style
The next major factor referred to the frequency with which respondents adopted the following management/supervisory styles at work: flexible; efficient; directive; authoritative; positive; sensitive, sympathetic; consultative, e.g. joint problem solving; co-operative, assertive; and dogmatic.

Type A coronary-prone behaviour
The final individual factor included in the multiple regression analysis was the score derived from the Bortner and Rosenman's (1967) adapted scale measuring coronary-prone Type A behaviour.

Health measures

The aim of the multiple regression analysis was to identify those sources of work stress and personality/behaviour factors that could predict risk to general ill-health, cigarette consumption, alcohol consumption, job dissatisfaction, and detrimental work performance. These health measures are discussed briefly below.

General health
The total health score assessed from the modified version of the Gurin Psychosomatic Symptom List (Gurin, *et al.* 1960) was the variable included. The potential range of scores was 25–107, extremely good to extremely poor health.

Cigarette consumption
Cigarette consumption rate was measured by the question requesting respondents to state the average number of cigarettes smoked a day. Seven categories were presented ranging from 0–5 cigarettes smoked a day to 40 plus a day.

Alcohol consumption
The factor chosen to measure alcohol consumption rates involved the question, 'Over the past year, which of the following best describes your typical drinking habits?' The six categorizations ranged from 'teetotal' to 'regularly more then 6 drinks a day' (one drink being a single whisky, gin, or brandy; a glass of wine, sherry, or port; or half a pint of beer).

Job satisfaction
In order to compute a single job satisfaction score, responses by each subject to the two job satisfaction items: 'I feel fairly well satisfied with my present job' and 'I find real enjoyment in my work', were summated. Respondents were asked to indicate which best described how they felt about their present job, using a 5-point Likert scale from 1 (strongly agree) to 5 (strongly disagree).

Work performance
The final health variable used in the regression analysis concerned work performance. A single work performance score was computed by summing the responses given by each subject to the 16 work performance items. Using the 5-point Likert scale from 1 (never) to 5 (always), respondents were asked how often they felt the following at work, e.g. 'unable to use my skills and knowledge', etc. Thus, the potential range of scores was from 16, indicating excellent overall job performance, to 80, very poor work performance.

The results

Female managers: general health score

Step-wise multiple regression analysis was calculated for the female managers' general health scores, with the work stress and personality/behaviour variables. It can be seen in Table 8.3 that there were five variables which significantly predict high psychosomatic health scores indicative of ill-health.

TABLE 8.3   PREDICTORS OF GENERAL ILL-HEALTH AMONG
FEMALE MANAGERS

Step	Variable	R Square	Simple R	Overall F	P
(1)	Factor 5 (workload)	0·101	0·317		
(2)	Factor 2 (Leadership/ authority role)	0·135	0·276		
(3)	Positive management style	0·160	−0·207		
(4)	Factor 3 (Home/partner relationships)	0·182	0·276		
(5)	Factor 6 (being single)	0·197	0·203	27·760	<0·001

R = correlation coefficient
F = regression ratio
P = statistical probability

It was of little surprise to discover the strong association between high work load/work pressures and ill-health,
as this substantiates numerous other studies which link
work overload with ill-health (French and Caplan, 1970;
Cooper 1981). A positive correlation was also found for the
second variable (factor 2) and ill-health. This factor constituted stress associated with female managers leadership/
authority role at work and included items concerning:
'managing/supervising people'; 'disciplining subordinates';
'being "the boss" '; 'working relationships with female
subordinates, female colleagues and male subordinates';
and 'playing the counsellor role at work'. The third predictor
of ill-health was almost certainly linked to stress associated with the authority role and was the negative
correlation between positive management style and ill-
health, i.e. frequently adopting a non-positive management
style was a predictor of ill-health.

The problems of adopting the appropriate management
style was reflected by two middle management women:

(1)   I find I have to walk a tightrope between retaining my
femininity, with a sensitive and sympathetic approach, and being a
tough, assertive and above all, unemotional manager. The thought

of being labelled a 'dragon' or a 'weak and emotional female' fills me with equal horror!

(2) I am aware that my lack of confidence and negative thinking prevent me from being happy in my career, but lack the decisiveness to move and have therefore adopted a *laissez-faire* attitude, lulled into apathy by the financial rewards of my present job.

Although I don't feel convinced I'm in the right job, or even the right career because I'm not actually *miserable* (all the time), I tend to think I should be grateful to be where I am, and have a job at all, so consequently feel guilty about being dissatisfied.

Many women managers also felt that the following positive management styles would be helpful, as outlined by a senior personnel manager:

Women must assert themselves; silence is too often taken as acquiescence in the expected role.

State her/your objectives – if you do not make your expectations known, you are not taken seriously.

Be polite and firm and refuse to be sidetracked, but avoid aggressive attitudes (she is aggressive, he is determined!).

Know your facts and never imply a knowledge you have not got.

The final two variables (factor 3 and factor 4), both involve stress associated with the home and social arena. Factor 3, labelled 'home/partner relationships', is made up of items concerning: 'demands of work on relationships with spouse/partner'; 'spouse/partner's attitude towards one's career'; 'lack of domestic and emotional support at home'; and 'earning more than one's spouse/partner'. Consequently, this confirms previous unproved suggestions that predictors of ill-health for female managers involve home/work conflicts as well as specific work stress factors (Cooper, 1982). This was further substantiated by the finding that factor 6, 'being single', was also a predictor of ill-health for women managers. This factor was formed using the two stress items related to 'being single and being sometimes excluded from social and business events such as dinner parties', and 'other people sometimes labelling one as a bit of an "oddity" '.

Male managers: general health score

Table 8.4 illustrates the results obtained from the step-wise multiple regression analysis for the male managers' general health scores with the work stress and personality/behaviour variables. Seven variables significantly predicted ill-health in male managers.

As with the female manager sample, a major variable emerging as a prominent predictor was the positive correlation between high work overload/time pressures (factor 3) and ill-health. Once again, this was an expected finding. In addition, lack of exercise and longer length of time in employment were found to be predictors of ill-health.

The two high job stress variables which evolved as predictors of ill-health in males, were concerned with organizational conflict and climate (factor 2) and feelings of overall alienation (factor 5). Certainly, organizational stressors stemming from role conflict, politics, lack of power and influence, poor communication and support from superiors have been suggested as predictors of ill-health in male management populations by numerous researchers (e.g. Cooper and Marshall, 1976), but these results empirically confirm these suspicions. The items forming factor 5 were not easily interpreted, and were given the vague label of 'alienation' as they included such items as 'business travel and staying in hotels alone', as well as 'being promoted beyond one's competence'. Whereas adopting a non-positive style of management was a predictor of ill-health for women managers, adopting a *dogmatic style* was related to ill-health in male managers.

Finally, unlike women managers, a high coronary Type A behaviour score emerged as a high health risk factor for males. This finding is in accordance with recent studies on male managers by such authors as Howard, *et al.* (1976), who found Type A male managers were higher on a number of risk factors associated with ill-health and CHD. Moreover, time pressures and work overload are stress factors often associated with Type A behaviour (Rosenman *et al.*, 1967), and one would have expected work overload

TABLE 8.4   PREDICTORS OF GENERAL ILL-HEALTH AMONG
MALE MANAGERS

Step	Variable	R Square	Simple R	Overall F	P
(1)	Factor 3 (workload)	0·069	0·263		
(2)	Exercise	0·128	0·235		
(3)	Factor 2 (the organization)	0·174	0·258		
(4)	Type A behaviour	0·209	0·240		
(5)	Dogmatic management style	0·225	0·156		
(6)	Years in lifetime employed full-time	0·241	0·137		
(7)	Factor 5 (alienation)	0·225	0·184	7·936	<0·001

pressures combined with Type A behaviour to have been two high-risk predictors of ill-health.

Besides the positive correlation between workload pressures and ill-health scores, the overall pattern of variables predicting ill-health differs for male managers and their female counterparts. *For men, the major predictors are not to do with home/career conflicts, but rather they concern job stressors stemming from organizational conflicts and alienation/isolation, being dogmatic, having little exercise, long years of employment and high Type A behaviour scores.*

Female managers: cigarette consumption

A regression analysis was carried out to identify whether any of the work stress variables were predictors of increased cigarette smoking in women managers. However, the results presented in table 8.5 show that although the five variables were highly significant, the amount of variance predicted was very small indeed. Consequently, as predictors of smoking behaviour, these variables need to be treated very cautiously. For example, firstly, there was a negative correlation between educational attainment and increased cigarette consumption, a finding which confirms Wingerson's (1981) review of smoking behaviour in women. Secondly, high Type A scores in women managers predicted

TABLE 8.5   FACTORS LEADING TO CIGARETTE CONSUMPTION IN
              FEMALE MANAGERS

Step	Variable	R Square	Simple R	Overall F	P
(1)	Educational attainment	0·024	−0·156		
(2)	Marital status	0·047	0·130		
(3)	Use humour	0·067	−0·146		
(4)	Type A behaviour	0·083	0·111		
(5)	Years in lifetime employed full-time	0·098	0·147	12·272	<0·001

increased cigarette consumption. Similar results emerged
from Howard's *et al.* (1976) examination of 236 male
managers. Other cigarette smoking risk factors for women
managers included being unattached, i.e. single, divorced/
separated or widowed, long years of employment, and
(surprisingly) using humour as a method of relaxation.

Male managers: cigarette consumption

An examination of table 8.6 reveals the seven variables
which significantly predicted high cigarette consumption in
male managers. Once again the amount of total variance
predicted was small and hence the variables cannot be
classified as statistically strong predictors of smoking
behaviour in males.

Nevertheless, as with female managers, a high Type A
score emerged as a predictor of high cigarette consumption
in male managers. Conversely, a negative relationship was
found between stress stemming from the leadership/author-
ity role (factor 1). Workload and time pressures (factor 3)
however, were the second major predictors of heavier
smoking in men, confirming earlier suggestions of this link
by such authors as Caplan, *et al.* (1975) and Ikard and
Tomkins (1973).

The other three variables which predicted increased
smoking in male managers all concerned management
styles. Male managers who adopted cooperative, directive

TABLE 8.6 FACTORS LEADING TO CIGARETTE CONSUMPTION
IN MALE MANAGERS

Step	Variable	R Square	Simple R	Overall F	P
(1)	Directive management style	0·057	0·239		
(2)	Factor 3 (workload)	0·092	0·177		
(3)	Company size	0·115	−0·194		
(4)	Type A behaviour	0·136	0·132		
(5)	Co-operative management style	0·152	0·141		
(6)	Flexible management style	0·173	−0·099		
(7)	Factor 1 (leadership/ authority role)	0·188	−0·034	5·362	<0·001

and non-flexible management styles smoked more cigarettes. As well, they were more likely to work in small organizations.

Female managers: alcohol consumption

Table 8.7 presents the three variables which were significantly related to alcohol consumption for female managers. With the small variance predicted, however, these variables cannot be viewed as stong predictors of increased alcohol consumption in women managers. The overall results suggest that women managers most at risk in relation to increased alcohol consumption are those in the higher levels of management, earning higher salaries, but not having been in full-time employment for a great number of years.

TABLE 8.7 FACTORS WHICH PREDICT HEAVY DRINKERS
AMONG FEMALE MANAGERS

Step	Variable	R Square	Simple R	Overall F	P
(1)	Management level	0·055	0·234		
(2)	Years in lifetime employed full-time	0·076	−0·118		
(3)	Annual salary	0·091	0·227	18·959	<0·001

Male managers: alcohol consumption

Regression analysis was also carried out to identify whether any of the work stress factors were predictors of increased alcohol consumption in male managers; the results are presented in table 8.8. Being unattached (i.e. single, divorced/separated or widowed), and Type A behaviour, emerge as major predictors. Once could suggest that the single male is more susceptible to feelings of isolation and lack of social/emotional support, and these are stress factors which have been previously isolated as precursors to increased alcohol drinking in men generally (Sargent, 1973). Further, increased drinking as a symptom of Type A behaviour, or vice versa, is an interesting result, as to date, few studies have either studied or found this association (Davidson and Cooper, 1980c).

Variables (3), (4) and (6) were to do with management styles and suggested that the adoption of flexible, non-dogmatic but non-consultative supervisory styles were predictors of alcohol consumption. Similarly, as with women managers, earning higher salaries correlated with heavier drinking. The other three predictors of drinking involved 'not using informal relaxation techniques', 'experiencing high pressure stemming from prejudice at work' (factor 6); and 'working in a predominantly female work environment'.

TABLE 8.8 FACTORS WHICH PREDICT HEAVY DRINKERS AMONG MALE MANAGERS

Step	Variable	R Square	Simple R	Overall F	P
(1)	Marital status	0·054	0·231		
(2)	Type A behaviour	0·086	0·172		
(3)	Flexible management style	0·127	0·173		
(4)	Consultative management style	0·153	−0·189		
(5)	Use informal relaxation techniques	0·176	0·145		
(6)	Dogmatic management style	0·199	−0·103		
(7)	Factor 6 (prejudice)	0·221	0·134		
(8)	Company gender constitution	0·238	−0·044		
(9)	Annual salary	0·265	0·133	6·400	<0·001

Female managers: job satisfaction

The fourth regression analysis aimed to identify predictor variables of job dissatisfaction. An examination of the results presented in table 8.9 shows that there were three variables which significantly predicted job dissatisfaction.

TABLE 8.9   WHAT MAKES A WOMAN MANAGER DISSATISFIED
WITH WORK?

Step	Variable	R Square	Simple R	Overall F	P
(1)	Factor 1 (The organization)	0·205	0·453		
(2)	Positive management style	0·246	−0·236		
(3)	Age	0·260	−0·220	62·426	<0·001

The major predictor of job dissatisfaction was experiencing 'high pressure linked to factors intrinsic to the organization' (factor 1). This factor included stress items such as: 'lack of support and encouragement from superiors'; 'inadequate supervision'; 'lack of communication, power, influence and control at work'; 'clarity of job role'; 'underpromotion'; 'inadequate work feedback'; 'feeling undervalued'; 'unclear career prospects'; 'office politics'; and 'beliefs conflicting with those of the organization'. Therefore, this factor included stress stemming from organizational structure and climate, role in the organization, as well as poor support from supervisors. These can best be summed up by a female junior manager:

I feel frustrated at not having the amount of responsibility at work which I feel I could cope with – partly due to my male boss being over-cautious in delegating problems to me as a female. If he had a male subordinate, I think he would 'favour' him.

As job satisfaction tends to increase with age (Caplan, et al. 1975), it was not surprising to find a negative correlation between age and job satisfaction, thus the younger woman manager tended to be most at risk in terms of job dissatisfaction. The final major predictor of job dissatisfaction was the adoption of a *non-positive* management style. This non-positive approach may reflect a less than positive self-image, as one woman production manager suggested:

I have worked with an outside consultant to develop my effectiveness in the face of sexual prejudice and occasional physical harassment. I have found that without a firm belief in my own ability the job would be more stressful. This work is still in process and will not be completed until Spring 1982, when I hope that many of my perceptions will be different and more positive than this has perhaps indicated. Above all else, I have learned not to compare myself favourably or unfavourably with others, but to recognize my worth as an individual.

In summary, the pattern which emerges for the woman manager at risk in relation to job dissatisfaction, is a younger woman experiencing pressure connected to poor organizational climate and poor supervision, together with a non-positive style of management.

Male managers: job satisfaction

Table 8.10 shows the results for male managers' job satisfaction scores with the stress variables. There were nine variables which significantly predicted job dissatisfaction. The same high risk characteristic emerged as a major predictor of job dissatisfaction for the male sample as it did for the female sample (i.e. high pressure associated with the organization, factor 2). In fact, the same nine items which formulated factor 2 in the factor analysis of the male stressors were also listed in the female managers' 'organization' factor (factor 1). Otherwise, the profile of the male manager at risk in terms of job dissatisfaction differed considerably to that of the female manager.

Somewhat surprisingly, the second major predictor of high job dissatisfaction was *low* home/work conflict and partner relationship pressures (factor 7). Once more, this confirms the general trend of our results over both Phase 1 and Phase 2 of our study, which indicates that male managers are far less affected by potential home and social pressures than their female counterparts.

TABLE 8.10 WHAT MAKES A MALE MANAGER DISSATISFIED WITH WORK?

Step	Variable	R Square	Simple R	Overall F	P
(1)	Factor 2 (The organization)	0·299	0·547		
(2)	Factor 7 (home/partner relationships)	0·324	−0·054		
(3)	Talk to someone you know	0·345	0·240		
(4)	Flexible management style	0·364	0·160		
(5)	Use humour	0·378	0·090		
(6)	Factor 1 (leadership/authority role)	0·388	0·014		
(7)	Efficient management style	0·403	−0·118		
(8)	Use relaxation techniques	0·414	−0·128		
(9)	Annual salary	0·425	−0·103	12·093	<0·001

However, certain patterns developed in connection with the adoption of relaxation techniques and management styles, and job dissatisfaction. Frequently, adopting 'relaxation techniques such as meditation and yoga', but not 'using humour' or 'talking to someone you know', were high risk behaviours in relation to job dissatisfaction. As well, job dissatisfaction was correlated with a *flexible* but *non-efficient* management style, and experiencing high pressure from items related to the leadership/authority role inherent in the job of management (factor 1). Finally, job dissatisfaction was negatively correlated with annual salary and this substantiates results from previous studies of male managers (e.g. Cooper and Marshall, 1976). In addition, high pressure scores stemming from rates of pay was a common complaint from male managers occupying all levels of the managerial hierarchy.

The profile that has formed for the male manager at risk of feeling high job dissatisfaction, involves high pressure stemming from organizational and leadership/authority role factors; experiencing low home/work pressures; adopting relaxation techniques but failing to use humour or talk to people in order to relax; using a flexible but non-efficient style of managing; and being dissatisfied with pay.

Female managers: work performance

The final analysis of stress variables was carried out against the overall work performance index for the female manager sample as a whole. As may be seen in table 8.11, six variables were isolated as being significant predictors of poor performance at work. Interestingly, three of these predictors were the adoption of specific management styles at work, i.e. non-positive, non-directive and non-efficient behaviours.

Logically, the second major predictor of poor work performance stemmed from high pressure inherent in the leadership/authority role (factor 2), a factor undoubtedly integrated with supervisory behaviour. The third predictor concerned high stress related to 'the organization' (factor 1). Factor 1 for the female sample constituted items such as 'poor supervision', 'lack of support and encouragement from superiors', 'beliefs conflicting with those of the organization' and so on. A final and unusual high risk variable involved a negative correlation between number of children and poor work performance.

TABLE 8.11   FACTORS RELATED TO POOR WORK PERFORMANCE
OF FEMALE MANAGERS

Step	Variable	R Square	Simple R	Overall F	P
(1)	Positive management style	0·179	−0·423		
(2)	Factor 2 (leadership/ authority role)	0·270	0·368		
(3)	Factor 1 (the organization)	0·315	0·321		
(4)	Directive management style	0·341	−0·346		
(5)	Number of children	0·354	−0·208		
(6)	Efficient management style	0·367	−0·360	54·520	<0·001

Thus, for the woman manager the pattern which has formed as a predictor of poor work performance, is one of a non-positive, non-directive and non-efficient management style, suffering high pressure in relation to her leadership/authority role and poor organizational structure and climate, and she is likely to have few children, if any at all.

It is most important, therefore, for women managers to take the advice of two successful women personnel managers:

(1) Being a woman means that impressions are most important – you always have to look capable even when inside you are feeling anything but. Extroverts are usually front-runners for management positions as females. You have to be *noticed* to be seen to exist.

I started in Personnel as a secretary and got rapid promotion because:

(1) I was qualified in IPM,
(2) I was willing to work hard and beyond my role as secretary;
(3) Despite a complete lack of any work experience worth mentioning, I became a Personnel Assistant in six months and a Personnel Officer eight months after that.

(2) I think that the main qualities and skills needed to survive are the ones we are inbuilt with; lack of natural arrogance is our biggest fault. Supreme confidence is a pre-requisite in most management positions. Women must learn to develop this as it is a very seductive quality.

Male managers: work performance

Table 8.12 highlights the sources of stress among male managers at work. Eleven variables significantly predict poor work performance.

As with the female managers, management style behaviour emerged as the common high risk item in terms of detrimental work performance. Nonetheless, with the exception of the adoption of a non-positive management style which was the major high risk predictor in both females and male managers, the other high risk management styles were different in men managers. They included frequently using non-authoritative, dogmatic, non-consultative, and non-flexible management styles.

Female and male managers also shared the second high risk variable relating to poor work performance, i.e. leadership/authority role pressures (factor 1). Likewise, high stress associated with organizational structure and climate

TABLE 8.12   FACTORS RELATED TO POOR WORK PERFORMANCE
OF MALE MANAGERS

Step	Variable	R Square	Simple R	Overall F	P
(1)	Positive management style	0·187	−0·432		
(2)	Factor 1 (leadership/authority role)	0·244	0·332		
(3)	Authoritative management style	0·276	−0·318		
(4)	Dogmatic management style	0·313	0·067		
(5)	Factor 2 (the organization)	0·334	0·317		
(6)	Marital status	0·348	0·086		
(7)	Exercise	0·359	−0·069		
(8)	Type A behaviour	0·370	0·098		
(9)	Consultative management style	0·382	−0.024		
(10)	Use humour	0·395	0·157		
(11)	Flexible management style	0·410	0·022	9.974	<0·001

(factor 2) were also predictors of impaired work performance at work for men managers. Other predictors which
were unique to the male sample were being 'unattached'
i.e. either single, divorced/separated or widowed (a major
high risk factor for high alcohol consumption in men
managers), and frequently taking exercise as a form of relaxation but rarely using humour. As well, male managers with a
high Type A coronary-prone behaviour score were high risk in
terms of detrimental work performance scores, a finding
which confirms the authors' review of Type A behaviour in the
work environment (Davidson and Cooper, 1980c).

In summary therefore, one can propose that the male
manager most at risk when it comes to detrimental performance at work, is a man who adopts non-positive, non-
authoritative, dogmatic, non-consultative, and non-flexible
management styles. He suffers from pressure linked to his
leadership/authority role and poor organizational climate
and structure in which he works. He is likely to be
unmarried, be Type A, and use exercise but not humour as a
coping strategy.

CHAPTER 9

Summary of findings: what can be done?

So far we have presented a detailed analysis and discussion of the quantitative results of our study; the aim of this chapter is to present an overall summary of the results with the aid of comprehensive models and figures. Significant higher sources of stress and their effect upon the health of female managers, compared with male managers, and vice versa, will be discussed. In addition, high stress factors and high stress outcomes for female and male managers, along with high risk profiles in relation to ill-health, cigarette smoking, alcohol consumption, job dissatisfaction and poor work performance, will be summarized. Finally, the research implications of the study will be presented with special emphasis on the training needs and organizational policy changes.

Summary of the problem areas for women and men managers

Figure 9.1 shows the sources of work stress that are problems for women in contrast to men managers while figure 9.2 indicates those that are difficulties for male as opposed to female managers. First, one can quickly con-clude after an examination of these figures that for both work stressor and health outcome variables, female mana-gers reported a far greater number of stress factors than their male counterparts. Therefore, while all these stress precursors and manifestations were not all necessarily 'high' stressors or 'high' stress outcomes, assessed cumulatively, *women in management are experiencing higher pressure*

FIGURE 9.1   A MODEL OF OCCUPATIONAL STRESS IN FEMALE MANAGERS: STATISTICALLY SIGNIFICANT HIGHER MEAN SCORES FOR FEMALE MANAGERS COMPARED WITH MALE MANAGERS

* $P<0.05$ ** $P<0.01$ *** $P<0.001$

| WORK ARENA | HOME AND SOCIAL ARENA | INDIVIDUAL ARENA |

Demographics
*** Lower management level
*** Lower salary
*** Fewer years worked full-time
*** Discontinuous work profile
*** Greater number of years break from workforce
*** Worked part-time
*** Being first of sex to hold job title
** Larger company

Factors intrinsic to the job
*** Business travel and staying in hotels alone
* Having to stand on feet all day

The token woman
*** Lack of same sex role models
*** Sex stereotyping role imposition
*** Performance pressure

Career development
*** Sex a disadvantage *re* job promotion/ career prospects
*** Sex discrimination and prejudice
*** Inadequate job training experience compared with colleagues of opposite sex
*** Colleagues of opposite sex treated more favourably by management

Relationships at work
*** Members of opposite sex seem uncomfortable working with me because of my sex

*** Fewer children
*** Earning more than spouse/partner
*** Dependants (other than children) living at home
*** Lack of domestic support at home
*** Conflicting responsibilities associated with running a home and career
*** Being single and labelled an 'oddity'
*** Being single and sometimes excluded from social and business events
Career-related dilemma concerning:
** whether to start a family
* whether to marry/ live with someone
** Lack of emotional support at home
* Fewer dependants living at home

Behaviour
Management styles:
* less flexible
* Higher Type A coronary-prone behaviour scores

FIGURE 9.1   (*continued*)

WORK ARENA	HOME AND SOCIAL ARENA	INDIVIDUAL ARENA

```
        Experiencing prejudiced
          attitudes at work
          because of my sex
          from members of:
***     the same sex
***     the opposite sex
*** Feeling uncomfortable
          on training courses
          when a member of
          the minority sex
*** Sexual harassment
 ** Lack of encouragement
          from superiors
  * Lack of social support
          from people at work
```

STRESS OUTCOMES

Psychosomatic symptoms	*Work performance*
*** Nervousness, tenseness	*** Lack confidence in putting forward my point of view
*** Headaches	*** Unable to be successful
*** Tiredness	*** Unable to cope well in conflict situations
*** Difficult to get up in morning	*** Reacting too emotionally to work problems
*** Cry easily	*** Lack self-confidence in ability to do my job
*** Spells of dizziness	* Unable to sell myself in competitive situations
*** Nightmares	
** Not eating	
** Want to be left alone	
* Mentally exhausted	
*** Total psychosomatic ill-health score	

levels stemming from stressors in the work, home/social and individual arenas, and more manifestations of psychosomatic symptoms and poorer work performance than are men managers.

A review of the high mean pressure scores reported by female managers in the work arena reveals interesting, if somewhat disturbing findings (see figure 9.1). Nearly every one of the 16 high pressure items categorized under 'factors intrinsic to the job', 'the token woman', 'career development', and 'relationships at work', were in some way associated with prejudice and sexual discrimination, coupled with being of the minority sex in a male-dominated occupation. Furthermore, this extended to demographic differences between female and male managers, with women usually being the first of their sex to hold their particular job title, at a lower managerial level, and earning a lower salary, than their male counterparts.

As two female top-level managers revealed:

(1)   As a woman I find the most irritating thing regarding men in business and their attitude towards me, is that if I should lose my temper they look knowingly at each other and mouth things to the effect of 'wrong time of the month!' – this has at least taught me to keep my temper!

(2)   The main problem and pressure of working in a managerial position in a predominantly male-orientated business is the need to prove everything twice over. One not only has to prove one's ability to do the job efficiently once, but twice, just in case the first time was pure luck. The only way I have found of dealing with this unfair discrimination is to smile patiently and furnish the necessary proof, however frustrating it may be!

In sum, the higher pressures at work to which female managers are being subjected, tend to be beyond their control, i.e. external discriminatory-based pressures. On the other hand, this is not the case for the male manager. Significantly higher pressure scores unique to the male manager compared with his female counterpart at work, involved pressure stemming from the leadership/authority aspects of management and rate of pay (even though his salary tends to be higher than his female colleagues) (see figure 9.2).

In the home and social arena, compared to men managers, women managers reported significantly higher pressure scores in respect to career and spouse/partner conflicts, career/home conflicts, and career and marriage/child bearing conflicts. Clearly, married women managers are still not getting the required emotional and domestic support from their partners. In addition, single women managers face higher pressures than their male counterparts in relation to

FIGURE 9.2 A MODEL OF OCCUPATIONAL STRESS IN MALE MANAGERS: STATISTICALLY SIGNIFICANT HIGHER MEAN SCORES FOR MALE MANAGERS COMPARED WITH FEMALE MANAGERS

* $P<0.05$ ** $P<0.01$ *** $P<0.001$

WORK ARENA / HOME AND SOCIAL ARENA / INDIVIDUAL ARENA

Demographics
*** Higher management level
*** Higher salary
*** Greater number of years worked full-time
*** Continuous work profile
*** Less number of years break from workforce
*** Not worked part-time
*** Not being first of sex to hold job title
** Smaller company

Factors intrinsic to the job
** Being the 'boss'
* Managing/supervising people
* Disciplining subordinates

Career development
* Rate of pay

*** More children
* More dependants living at home

Coping
** Less likely to talk to someone you know

Behaviour
Management style:
** less sensitive, sympathetic
** less cooperative
* less efficient

STRESS OUTCOMES

Psychosomatic symptoms
** Upset stomach

Work performance
* Unable to produce satisfactory quantity of work

Drug use
*** Alcohol consumption
* Have alcoholic drink to relax

feeling an 'oddity', being excluded from social/business events and career conflict over whether to marry/live with someone. As well, both married and single women managers reported higher pressure over their career-related dilemma concerning starting a family in the foreseeable future.

Not surprisingly, in the individual arena, women managers had significantly higher Type A coronary-prone behaviour scores. There was only one gender difference connected to coping strategies, with men managers being less likely to talk to someone they knew. Interestingly, while there was little overall difference in the frequency with which female and male managers maintained they adopted management styles, certain differences did emerge, especially for the male managers. While women managers less frequently adopted a flexible style of management, male managers reported using less frequently the efficient, sensitive/sympathetic and cooperative management styles, compared to their female counterparts.

As far as the manifestation of stress was concerned, female managers reported experiencing more often, a far greater number of psychosomatic symptoms (i.e. 10) in contrast to men (i.e. 1). The total mean psychosomatic ill-health score was significantly higher for the female manager sample. However, male managers drank more alcohol than did the female managers. The other stress outcome concerned poor work performance. Unfortunately, women managers reported significantly poorer work performance scores on six items compared to only one ('unable to produce satisfactory quantity of work') scored significantly higher by men. For women managers, the poor work performance factors were predominantly associated with lack of assertion and confidence – skills which undoubtedly require emphasis in future management training. In sum, after reviewing the comparative results highlighted in figures 9.1 and 9.2, one might conclude that, cumulatively, *women managers are experiencing significantly more pressure and a greater number of stress manifestations than are men managers.*

High stress factors and their outcomes for female and male managers

Figure 9.3 illustrates the high stress factors and their outcomes for female and male managers by level in the management hierarchy. A high stress factor constituted a mean pressure score of 2·5 or above (1=no pressure at all, to 5=a great deal of pressure) in response to job, organizational, home and social stress. The criteria selected to isolate a poor-health/well-being measure was a mean score of 2·5 or above in response to items listed in the General Health Questionnaire, job satisfaction, the use of drugs in order to relax, and work performance measures. With the exception of Type A behaviour, demographic and individual variables such as management styles, were not included. Alcohol and cigarette consumption were seen as high stress-related behaviours, if the consumption rates exceeded those isolated by other researchers using comparable populations.

An inspection of figure 9.3 reveals certain high stress factors and high stress outcomes which were common to both men and women occupying the same management level. In particular, *work overload* pressures were reported by men and women at all levels of the managerial hierarchy, with the exception of supervisors. The major stress factor common to men and women occupying all the managerial levels was associated with *time pressures and deadlines,* while middle managers and supervisors of both sexes experienced high pressure due to *lack of consultation and communication.*

When it came to high stress outcomes, females and males in senior, middle, junior and supervisory management positions, all reported smoking, drinking and eating too much; drinking coffee or Coke or eating in order to relax; and (with the exception of supervisors) having an alcoholic drink as a method of unwinding. Senior female and male managers and supervisors most often complained of tiredness and supervisors also found it difficult to get up in the morning and often wanted to be left alone. *Both male and female senior executives were highly susceptible to nervous-ness, feeling fidgety or tense.* Men and women in junior and middle management both seemed most at risk in relation to poor work performance. Junior managers of both sexes asserted that they were frequently unable to use their skills and knowledge and were unable to 'sell themselves' in competitive situations. Males and females at the middle management level maintained they frequently made mis-takes at work.

An investigation into the high stress factors and their outcomes unique to female and male managers exhibited in

FIGURE 9.3   HIGH STRESS FACTORS AND THEIR OUTCOMES
FOR FEMALE AND MALE MANAGERS
* P<0·05   ** P<0·01   *** P<0·001

FEMALES	FEMALES AND MALES	MALES

SENIOR MANAGERS

Lack of consultation/ communication Type A behaviour	Work overload Time pressures/ deadlines	** Underpromotion
OUTCOME	OUTCOME	OUTCOME
* Difficult to get up in morning Want to be left alone Smoking cigarettes	Nervousness, tenseness Tiredness Drink coffee, eat, in order to relax Smoke, drink, eat too much Have alcohol in order to relax	Making mistakes

MIDDLE MANAGERS

*** Feel have to perform better at job than colleagues of opposite sex *** Career-related dilemma concerning whether to start a family *** Type A behaviour	Work overload Time pressures/ deadlines Lack of consultation/ communication	* Rate of pay Sacking someone
OUTCOME	OUTCOME	OUTCOME
*** Unable to cope well in conflict situations *** Tiredness * Sleep trouble * Nervousness, tenseness * Difficult to get up in morning * Want to be left alone Unable to influence and persuade people Unable to 'sell myself' in competitive situations Smoking cigarettes	Smoke, drink, eat too much Drink coffee, eat, in order to relax Have alcohol in order to relax Making mistakes	Unable to use skills and knowledge

continues

FIGURE 9.3   (*continued*)

FEMALES	FEMALES AND MALES	MALES

JUNIOR MANAGERS

*** Sex a disadvantage *re* job promotion/career prospects	Work overload Time pressures/ deadlines	** Disciplining subordinates Sacking someone Underpromotion
** Office politics		
** Career-related dilemma concerning whether to start a family		
Type A behaviour		
Feeling undervalued		
Unclear career prospects		

OUTCOME	OUTCOME	OUTCOME

*** Nervousness, tenseness	Smoke, drink, eat too much	Unable to influence and persuade people
*** Tiredness	Drink coffee, eat, in order to relax	
* Difficult to get up in morning	Have alcohol in order to relax	
* Want to be left alone	Unable to use skills and knowledge	
* Unable to cope well in conflict situations	Unable to 'sell myself' in competitive situations	
Making mistakes		

SUPERVISORS

	Time pressures/ deadlines	** Long working hours
	Lack of consultation/ communication	Work overload
		Staff shortages/ turnover rate
		Equipment failures
		Unclear career prospects
		Rate of pay
		Redundancy threat

OUTCOME	OUTCOME	OUTCOME

Nervousness, tenseness	Tiredness	Sleep trouble
Headaches	Difficult to get up in morning	Job dissatisfaction.
Making mistakes	Smoke, drink, eat too much	
	Want to be left alone	
	Drink coffee, eat, in order to relax	

continues

FIGURE 9.3   (*continued*)

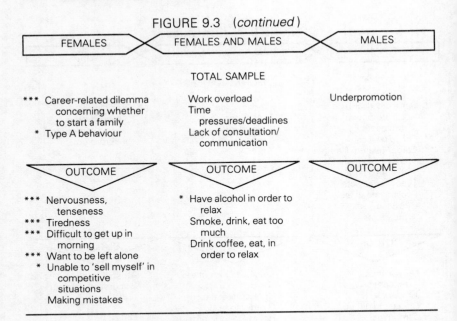

FEMALES	FEMALES AND MALES	MALES

TOTAL SAMPLE

*** Career-related dilemma
      concerning whether
      to start a family
  * Type A behaviour

Work overload
Time
      pressures/deadlines
Lack of consultation/
      communication

Underpromotion

OUTCOME · OUTCOME · OUTCOME

*** Nervousness,
      tenseness
*** Tiredness
*** Difficult to get up in
      morning
*** Want to be left alone
  * Unable to 'sell myself' in
      competitive
      situations
  Making mistakes

  * Have alcohol in order to
      relax
  Smoke, drink, eat too
      much
  Drink coffee, eat, in
      order to relax

figure 9.3, shows that with the exception of female supervisors, *women in junior, middle and senior management, are
experiencing a greater number of high stress factors and
manifestations than their male counterparts.* Moreover,
female supervisors, despite experiencing no unique high
stress factors, are, unlike male supervisors, susceptible to
nervousness, tenseness, headaches and making mistakes at
work. *High stress factors and their outcomes specific to senior
women executives involved lack of consultation and communication, Type A behaviour, wanting to be left alone,
smoking cigarettes and finding it difficult to get up in the
morning.* Undoubtedly, this latter stress outcome is linked
to their complaints of tiredness which were significantly
greater than those of senior male executives. In addition,
coronary-prone behaviour pattern Type A was also an
important precursor variable in female middle and junior
managers – characterized by extremes of haste, restlessness,
competitiveness, impatience and feelings of being under
pressure of time and under the challenge of responsibility.
There can be no doubt that *female middle and junior*

managers reported the greatest number of combined high stress factors and their outcomes in comparison with women or men occupying any of the other managerial levels. Unlike female senior executives who have successfully broken into the higher echelons of management, middle and junior management women reported high pressure associated with sexual discrimination and prejudice; this was true especially of women in junior levels. Middle management females complained of feelings of high pressure connected with having to perform better at their jobs than their male colleagues, and women junior managers suffered high pressure due to feeling their sex to be a disadvantage regarding job promotion, unclear career prospects, and feeling undervalued. Female junior managers were also bothered by office politics and shared the high pressure 'my career-related dilemma concerning whether to start a family', with female middle managers. These results imply that the woman junior manager views her sex as a major disadvantage in terms of her future career advancement prospects and this is a major source of stress to her.

Stress outcomes unique to both middle and junior female managers, but not shared with their male counterparts, include nervousness and tenseness, tiredness, difficulty in getting up in the morning and wanting to be left alone. Female middle managers are susceptible to sleep troubles and tend to be heavier smokers. Both middle and junior female managers reported poor work performance behaviours not shared with their male counterparts. For middle management females, these consisted of being frequently 'unable to influence and persuade people' 'unable to "sell oneself" in competitive situations', and 'unable to cope well in conflict situations'. This final poor work performance factor was also unique to female junior managers, in addition to frequently making mistakes.

In comparison to women managers, with the exception of male supervisors, there were relatively few high stress factors and their outcomes unique to male managers. For men in senior, middle and junior management, unique stress factors tended to concern underpromotion, sacking someone, disciplining subordinates and rate of pay. Interestingly, men in these three management levels isolated one different unique detrimental performance behaviour not shared with their female countemporaries: 'making mistakes' for senior male managers; 'unable to use my skills and knowledge' for middle management males; and 'unable to influence and persuade people', for junior male managers. On the other hand, in contrast to female supervisors, male supervisors complained of a number of unique high stress factors concerned with work overload and long working hours, rate of pay, staff shortages, equipment failures, unclear career prospects and redundancy threats. Unlike female supervisors, they complained of sleep troubles and were the only management category of either females or males to report high job dissatisfaction.

Looking at the total sample of male managers, a high unique stress factor is related to male managers feeling they are underpromoted and employed beneath their competence (a result which would appear to confirm Harlan and Weiss's (1980) finding that male managers have higher aspiration levels than their female counterparts). Conversely, women managers overall exhibit Type A behaviour and experience high pressure in their career-related dilemma concerning whether to start a family. They also suffer four unique psychosomatic ill-health symptoms not shared with male managers: nervousness; tenseness; tiredness and difficulty in getting up in the morning; and often wanting to be left alone. They also complain of being unable to 'sell themselves' in competitive situations, and of making mistakes.

In conclusion, by summing the total high stress factor and their outcomes of women and men working in each of the managerial levels, it is possible to present a hierarchical list of management populations most 'at risk' in the context of 'occupational stress'. Women in junior and middle management experience the highest overall 'occupational stress' levels, followed by male supervisors, senior women managers, male junior managers, female supervisors and male middle managers, and finally senior male managers, who report the lowest 'occupational stress' levels. Moreover, the total female management sample reported 50 per cent more combined high stress factors and their outcomes in comparison with those reported by the total male management sample.

Stress vulnerability profiles

Figure 9.4 exhibits the stress vulnerability profiles of female and male managers most 'at risk' of showing symptoms of stress, i.e. ill-health, cigarette smoking, alcohol

FIGURE 9.4   STRESS VULNERABILITY PROFILES IN FEMALE AND MALE MANAGERS

WORK ARENA	HOME AND SOCIAL ARENA	INDIVIDUAL ARENA

JOB DISSATISFACTION

	Work Arena	Home and Social Arena	Individual Arena
Female	Organizational climate pressures		Non-positive management style Younger age
Male	Organizational climate pressures Leadership/authority role pressures Lower salary	Home/partner relationships – *low* pressure	Not talk to someone to relax Flexible management style Not use humour to relax Non-efficient management style Using relaxation techniques

POOR WORK PERFORMANCE

	Work Arena	Home and Social Arena	Individual Arena
Female	Leadership/authority role pressures Organizational climate pressures	Few (if any) children	Non-positive management style Non-directive management style Non-efficient management style
Male	Leadership/authority role pressures Organizational climate pressures	Unmarried	Non-positive management style Non-authoritative management style Dogmatic management style Exercise frequently Type A Non-consultative management style Not using humour to relax Flexible management style

FIGURE 9.4   (*continued*)

WORK ARENA	HOME AND SOCIAL ARENA	INDIVIDUAL ARENA

ILL-HEALTH

	WORK ARENA	HOME AND SOCIAL ARENA	INDIVIDUAL ARENA

Female	Workload pressures
	Leadership/authority
	    pressures
		Home/partner
		    relationship pressures
		'Being single' pressures
			Non-positive management
			    style

Male	Long years of
	    employment
	Workload pressures
	Organizational climate
	    pressures
	Alienation pressures
			Little exercise
			Type A
			Dogmatic management
			    style

CIGARETTE SMOKING

	WORK ARENA	HOME AND SOCIAL ARENA	INDIVIDUAL ARENA

Female	Long years of
	    employment
		Unmarried	Lower educational
			    attainment
			Use humour to relax
			Type A

Male	Workload pressures
	Small organization
	Leadership/authority
	    role: *low* pressures
			Directive management
			    style
			Type A
			Co-operative management
			    style
			Non-flexible management
			    style

ALCOHOL DRINKING

	WORK ARENA	HOME AND SOCIAL ARENA	INDIVIDUAL ARENA

Female	High management
	    level
	Few years of
	    employment
	Higher salary
		Unmarried	

Male	Prejudice pressures
	Female-dominated work
	    environment
	Higher salary
			Type A
			Flexible management style
			Non-consultative
			    management style
			Not using informal
			    relaxation techniques
			Non-dogmatic
			    management style

consumption, job dissatisfaction, and poor work performance. (These 'high risk' profiles were formulated by using
step-wise multiple regression analysis.)

From figure 9.4, certain general findings emerge. First,
the stress vulnerability profiles of female versus male
managers for each of the five stress symptoms, are on the
whole, quite different. In fact, the only real similar 'high
risk' profiles of both female and male managers, is the one
'at risk' of producing poor work performance. Second, the
strongest predictive risk variables for both female and male
managers were found in the analysis of the relationships
between the stress factors and job dissatisfaction and
detrimental work performance. Consequently, this implies
that other manifestations of ill-health – cigarette smoking
and alcohol drinking – not included in the questionnaire,
were important predictors of these stress symptoms.

In relation to psychosomatic ill-health, an obvious
relevant variable not included in this study is the subject's
genetic susceptibility to illness. In Davidson's study of
occupational stress in police for example, she compared her
subject's family history of certain illnesses with census
statistics of illness in a matched population, and found her
police subjects to be a very 'high risk' population in terms of
their genetic susceptibility to certain illnesses such as coronary heart disease (Davidson and Veno, 1980).

Possibly, the exclusion of personality inventory in this
study may have contributed to the relatively weak predictive
power of our stress variables with cigarette and alcohol
consumption rates. Indeed, other authors have found strong
correlations between such personality traits as neuroticism
and anxiety, and increased smoking and alcohol drinking
(McCrae, Costa and Bosse, 1978; Cooper and Melhuish,
1980). One also needs to consider the increasing social
pressure to stop or cut down smoking, and heavy drinking in
females is still socially frowned upon. Finally, it is of interest
to note that, with the exception of female senior managers
who tend to be heavier drink consumers of alcohol, management level did not emerge as a 'high risk' predictor for any of
the stress symptoms in either the female or the male
samples.

ILL-HEALTH: 'HIGH-RISK' PROFILES OF FEMALE AND MALE MANAGERS

The woman manager most 'at risk' in relation to psychosomatic ill-health symptoms is someone who at work is subjected to high pressure associated with heavy workloads, and who finds the job functions connected with her leadership/authority role very stressful. In addition, she often adopts a non-positive management style. At home, she is also suffering high pressure, especially with her partner, due to his lack of support. If she is single, she also feels the additional pressure due to being labelled a bit of 'an oddity' and being excluded from social and business functions.

The profile of the 'high risk' illness-prone, male manager is somewhat different. He is likely to have been working full-time for quite a number of years. In the work environment, he is subjected to high workload pressures, but also experiences high stress due to factors related to the organizational climate and structure in which he works. He tends to feel alienated at work and frequently adopts a dogmatic style of management. This male manager will have a Type A coronary-prone behaviour pattern, and will take little exercise.

CIGARETTE SMOKERS: 'HIGH RISK' PROFILES OF FEMALE AND MALE MANAGERS

The female manager who is most likely to be a heavy smoker has been in full-time employment for a greater number of years and has few educational qualifications. She is probably not married, i.e. she is either single, divorced/separated or widowed, has a Type A behaviour pattern and will often resort to using humour as a method of relaxation.

The heavy smoker male manager, on the other hand, experiences high workload pressures, works in a small organization and experiences little stress in relation to his leadership/authority role as a manager. While his management style is often directive and cooperative, it is also non-flexible. Like female managers who smoke a lot, he is also Type A.

ALCOHOL DRINKERS: 'HIGH RISK' PROFILES OF FEMALE AND MALE MANAGERS

The woman in management who drinks most alcohol has spent relatively few years in full-time employment and yet she has managed to work her way up quickly to the higher senior levels of management; at the same time, she enjoys a high salary.

While heavy drinking male managers also earn high salaries, unlike their female counterparts, they experience high pressuress at work due to prejudice and they work in predominantly female environments. Perhaps this finding is indicative of 'token men' in female work environments being subjected to the same prejudice pressures usually reserved for 'token women'! This male manager is likely to be unmarried, i.e. single, divorced/separated, widowed; and have a Type A behaviour pattern. The male heavy drinker is also likely to use a flexible, non-consultative but non-dogmatic supervisory style; he rarely uses informal relaxation methods.

JOB DISSATISFACTION: 'HIGH RISK' PROFILES OF FEMALE AND MALE MANAGERS

The woman manager most 'at risk' in feeling high levels of job dissatisfaction is one who experiences high pressure due to stress factors inherent in the organizational structure and climate in which she works. She will frequently adopt a non-positive management style at work. She is likely to be quite young.

Similarly, the male manager most likely to be experiencing job dissatisfaction also suffers from high pressures linked to organizational structure and climate. However, he also experiences high stress stemming from factors intrinsic in the leadership/authority role he has to play at work. He will be earning a low salary and adopt a flexible but also non-efficient management style. Even though the dissatisfied male manager will frequently use relaxation techniques such as meditation and yoga, he will rarely talk to people or use humour as forms of relaxation. Home and social stress factors have little influence on job dissatisfaction for either female or male managers. In fact, the highly dissatisfied male manager experiences very low home/partner relationship pressures.

POOR WORK PERFORMANCE: 'HIGH RISK' PROFILES OF FEMALE AND MALE MANAGERS

The female manager most 'at risk' in performing poorly at work is a woman experiencing high pressure at work in relation to the leadership/authority role functions and from the organizational structure and climate in which she works. She frequently behaves in a non-positive, non-directive and non-efficient management style. She is unlikely to have many (if any) children.

Likewise, the male manager most likely to perform badly at work also experiences high stress connected to leadership/authority role pressures and organizational structure and climate pressures, and he frequently adopts a non-positive management style. In addition, he tends to be non-authoritative, flexible but also non-consultative and dogmatic, in the way he manages people at work. Although he is Type A, he frequently exercises. He rarely uses humour as a form of relaxation and is likely to be unmarried, i.e. single, divorced/separated or widowed.

Organizational and policy changes

The results of our study are *not* meant to give ammunition to any potential employers of female managers – indeed the findings indicate that women who break into middle and senior levels of management have often had to be better at their job and better at coping with stress than their male colleagues. As well, there appears to be very little difference in the management styles adopted by male and female managers, if anything men maintain they use more negative management styles than do women.

Many of the female managers interviewed by the authors suggested that major changes are necessary to herald 'real' equal opportunities at work. These changes will have to take into account the educational system, the socialization process, government policy and political awareness. We agree with the propositions in a report by The Industrial Society (1980) which recommended the following action:

(1) Stimulate industry into encouraging able women to take up careers in management and improve, therefore, attitudes among parents, teachers and women generally.

(2) Ensure that girls are given guidance and opportunities at schools and in higher education.

(3) Reduce sex bias in education and particularly in subject choice.

Our research has shown that women managers are more likely to be single than are men managers, and therefore *often do not have the domestic and social support of a spouse* at home. On the other hand, *the married women managers usually spend far more hours on house/child care duties* compared with their husbands and married male managers. Thus, we support Virginia Novarra's (1980) assertion that: 'a major factor inhibiting progress towards equal opportunity is the extremely low levels of participation by men, and boys, in domestic tasks and child-care within the family' (p. 100).

The other disturbing findings which emerge from this study centre on the overwhelming evidence that the *majority of additional pressures at work experienced by female managers are stress factors beyond their control* and *based largely on prejudice and discrimination from both organizational/ corporate policy and other people at work*. Therefore, if one takes a future comparative prognosis of a young male and female junior manager – in the majority of organizations in this country, the dice is already heavily loaded against the woman in terms of salary, career development, and promotion. It is not surprising that very few women reach senior management positions in Britain. What is clear from our study is that the majority of organizations appear to be ensuring that management (especially higher level management) remains a *male*-dominated preserve. Organizations have to acknowledge the fact that more women are entering management – especially at the graduate level. At the moment, *these women are not being given the same equal opportunities to develop a career in management as their male counterparts. Hence this is an enormous loss to organizations, both in terms of economic and management talents.* It is therefore, incumbent on *all* organizations to develop corporate personnel policies that will minimize the numerous barriers, which this study has found to be particularly operative against women managers. It is also important that companies acknowledge the reality of dual-career managerial couples and families, and that they try to accommodate them.

In order to achieve a more equitable working climate, we would recommend the following policy changes.

Affirmative action
If the position of women in management in this country is to improve, we believe there is a need for stronger legislative/legalistic programmes to force equal opportunities. Britain should consider adopting the US approach of 'affirmative action', whereby organizations who receive government grants or loans or contracts, etc. must follow a positive recruitment strategy toward the employment of women and minority groups, or lose their government award. It is important to note that research has shown that affirmative action policies also help to change attitudes, e.g. male managers who have worked with women in senior management, compared with those who have not.

Affirmative action policy and activities
Until legislative changes occur, organizations themselves should develop their own equal opportunities guidelines and affirmative action policies which provide women in management with career opportunities, such as career planning and counselling, the creation of informal support networks for all women managers, helping male managers to come to terms with women managers and providing senior management sponsorship, etc.

By 1978, an Equal Opportunities Commission survey of current practices of 500 leading UK companies revealed that only 25 per cent had formal policy statements, although most did not have associated action plans to implement them. Some companies, like ICI had surveyed their pattern of female employment and issued a code of practice to improve job appraisal and training for women, which it is anticipated may increase the number of female managers at middle and senior levels over the next few years. It is particularly important that women managers are allowed equal training opportunities, taking into account that the women managers in our study complained of inadequate training compared to their male colleagues.

Organizations should follow the example of the Greater London Council and Thames Television which have appointed their own Equal Opportunities Committees and Advisers. Six months after the appointment of a women's employment officer at Thames Television, for example, management training to avoid sex discrimination was started. A new booklet on non-discriminatory codes of practice for interviewing has now been produced. Financial assistance for day care is now offered to male and female employees and crèches are to be introduced. A company profile of staff is also being completed. Thames TV's women's employment officer is also backed by a 'positive action committee'.

Unions
Union officials should take active steps in promoting equal opportunities for women at work. Information should be demanded from employers in order to assess what jobs women do. Inequalities should be researched (e.g. the survey of sexual harassment at work carried out by NALGO), and problems tackled effectively. Women should also be encouraged to stand for office in their union in order to break the male monopoly of workers' interests. In addition, unions should consider seriously an affirmative action policy regarding the proportion of appointed female union officials.

Maternity and paternity leave
With women managers at all levels of the managerial
hierarchy reporting the major pressure of their career being
the dilemma whether or not to start a family, reasonable
maternity *and* paternity leave is required, with a guaranteed
right to return to work and some financial security during the
leave period. Paternity leave is particularly important in the
changing circumstances of the family and may enourage
husbands of women managers to give more emotional and
domestic support in the home. In Sweden, for example, a
couple are financially penalized if fathers *do not* take a
minimum stipulated paternity leave. Few organizations in
this country provide this contemporary innovation, but
many will have to consider it in the near future if they want
to avoid problems of uncontrolled absenteeism.

Day nursery facilities
The number of places in UK local government day nurseries
were 22,000 in 1961, increasing only to 30,000 in 1980. Until
governments take over the responsibility of providing day
nurseries it appears that organizations will have to take the
initiative themselves, by offering financial assistance for day
care to both male and female employees and introducing
crèches.

Retraining schemes
Many women who wish to return to the workforce after a
number of years away, often lack confidence and feel that
they are out of date. It is in the interest of employers and the
wider community to provide opportunities for such women
to be brought up to date with current developments. This
might best be done by professional associations, or indeed
by work organizations providing updating courses for ex-
employees who have temporarily left employment to raise a
family.

Flexible working agreements
There is a wide range of flexible working arrangements
which organizations can offer their female and male

employees, and which may help changing family patterns. Such arrangements include *flexi-time, part-time work* and *job sharing*. Moreover, with the advent of the microprocessor revolution, it should become increasingly easier for dual career husbands and wives, in certain types of jobs, to work at home.

Change in relocation policies
Both women and men managers should be allowed the opportunity of promotion without moving.

Training implications

A number of implications for future management training emerge from the results of this study. It was found that 22 per cent of the interview sample were absolutely against 'female only' training courses of any kind, believing them to be a form of discrimination via segregation, and arguing that such courses would be too far removed from the real world of organizations. Nevertheless, the majority of this sample conceded that 'all-female management training courses probably had benefits, especially for women just beginning a career in management' (see table 9.1).

The data collected from the women manager interviewees supports the contention that foundation stones of social skill training were in the areas of 'confidence building' and 'being more assertive'. (The assertive person, according to Alberti and Emmons (1970) is ' . . . open and flexible, genuinely concerned with the rights of others, yet at the same time able to establish very well his or her own rights'.)

We asked the female interviewees what managerial skills they would like to develop. Table 9.2 lists these major skills broken down by levels in the managerial hierarchy. It seems that senior female managers are more concerned with interpersonal skills of managing people, dealing with men at work more successfully, as well as task skills of learning about new technology and being able to retain more information. Middle and junior managers, on the other hand, appeared to want to learn how to cope with their role

TABLE 9.1   THE FEMALE MANAGERS' INTERVIEW SAMPLE:
THE TRAINING WE NEED

Type of training	Percentage of total sample
Confidence building	50
Assertion	42
Interpersonal skills	12
General management skills, including delegation, disciplining, negotiating	10
Learning to cope with men at work including sex role stereotyping imposition	8
Political awareness	7
Training for men to cope with women	6
Desocializing *re:* sex stereotyping	5
Leadership	5
Retraining for women entering workforce	3
Personal presentation	3
Power of speech and public speaking	3
Resilience	2
How to do well at interviews	2

as a woman manager, dealing with difficult staff (particularly men), delegation, assertiveness, and being more persuasive. Supervisory managers seemed to be interested in developing the basic skills of management, such as understanding finance, new technology, administration, etc.

The future management training implications which emerge from the results of the larger *questionnaire survey sample,* centre largely on the types of management styles adopted by women and men managers and their detrimental work performance ratings. An examination of the 'stress vulnerability profiles' clearly illustrates the negative consequences in terms of stress outcomes when both women and men in management frequently adopt negative management styles. *Even so, it appears that, overall, men managers practise negative management styles more often than their female counterparts.* While women tend to be less flexible, male managers are more likely to adopt less efficient, less sensitive and sympathetic, and less cooperative management styles. Therefore, future management training for both men

TABLE 9.2   THE FEMALE MANAGER INTERVIEW SAMPLE:
TRAINING SKILLS WE WOULD LIKE TO DEVELOP

Senior managers
Managing people generally
How to deal with men at work more successfully
Putting over a less superficial attitude – people often don't know if I
    mean what I say
Keeping up with new technology
Learning not to take on so much
Consulting skills
Skim reading

Middle managers
Dealing with difficult staff, especially men
Assertion skills
Delegation
How to be taken more seriously, as a woman
Disciplining

Junior managers
Being labelled 'the boss'
Assertion and confidence
Delegation
Training abilities and assertion
Managing more people

Supervisors
Finance and budgeting
Economics
Administration
More mechanical training
More technical training

and women should highlight and remedy these managerial
weaknesses in both sexes.

In table 9.3, the poor work performance behaviour for
females and males in management level terms and overall,
have been isolated. (Poor work performance is defined in
terms of a mean score of 2·5 or above (1=never to
5=always) in response to the question 'How often do you
feel the following at work?') *Junior and middle managers* of
both sexes report most work performance difficulties and
these are mainly associated with lack of confidence, assertion and general business skills and knowledge. At the

TABLE 9.3 POOR WORK PERFORMANCE IN FEMALE AND
MALE MANAGERS

Females	Females and males	Males
Middle managers Unable to 'sell myself' in competitive situations***	Making mistakes	Unable to use skills and knowledge
Unable to influence and persuade people		
Junior managers Unable to cope well in conflict situations*	Unable to use skills and knowledge	Unable to influence and persuade people
Making mistakes	Unable to 'sell myself' in competitive situations	
Supervisors Making mistakes		
Total sample Unable to 'sell myself' in competitive situations*		
Making mistakes		

   * $P<0.05$
  ** $P<0.01$
*** $P<0.001$

middle management level, however, *men complain of business skill deficits,* that is, of making mistakes and being unable to use their skills and knowledge. Women, however, are still maintaining they have a combination of underdeveloped business skills and confidence and assertion skills; they complain of 'making mistakes', 'being unable to influence and persuade people', and 'being unable to "sell themselves" in competitive situations'.

Senior female managers and male supervisors reported no major work performance difficulties while senior male executives and female supervisors maintained they often made mistakes. For the total male management sample, no detrimental work peformance behaviours emerged constituting a mean score of 2·5 or above. On the other hand, the total female management sample reported being often 'unable to sell themselves in competitive situations', and often 'making mistakes'.

Many women find it difficult to persuade their firms to send them on training courses, as this production manager suggests:

I have found this company unwilling to send me on management (as opposed to Technical) training, or on courses specifically for women managers, where such problems as women managers experience might be dealt with and discussed rather than denied.
I have paid for and attended two of the Industrial Society Saturday development courses. These have been of tremendous benefit to me because it is a great relief to meet other women managers and find that *they have exactly the same problems*. I feel less of a freak – I'm not imagining it all. I also feel less isolated – there are other women managers out there somewhere!

Even when women managers are given the opportunity, not enough of them are trained on entering a 'man's world', as this female middle manager suggests:

I strongly feel that the training required for women entering management areas should be centred not only on the specific skills for the job in question, but also on the essential theme that they are entering a 'man's world', and in order to compete on equal terms must develop a mental attitude that gives them the confidence to deal with senior male managers on equal terms. I am not suggesting that they should relinquish their outward feminine appearance, but they cannot expect to rely on tears or any other feminine wiles to overcome difficult problems or situations.

The results of this study also clearly indicate that there is an obvious need for the introduction of more Type A behaviour modification programmes both for female and male managers. There have been fears expressed – particularly by Type A individuals – that if there are large-scale attempts to change Type As into practising Type Bs, this will adversely affect not only the socio-economic well-being of the individuals involved, but also the country's overall quality and quantity of work output (Cooper and Marshall, 1978). However, evidence obtained from Type A behaviour modification programmes and clinical observations indicates that these fears are unfounded. Friedman and Rosenman (1974) assert that Type B individuals are just as likely to be as ambitious and intelligent as their Type A counterparts. Moreover, unlike Type As, Type Bs seem to be able to express their drive through security and confidence, rather than irritation and annoyance.

Chesney and Rosenman (1980) have shown that Type A behaviour change programmes, with both coronary heart disease patients and healthy subjects, have led to significant declines in serum cholesterol levels and blood pressures, lowered frequencies of subsequent coronary events, increased work productivity and improved family relationships. Furthermore, they have emphasized the importance of training individuals at the same time to maximize their work performance.

In an attempt to change a Type A's style of living, these modification programmes involve such exercises as relaxation (both physical and cognitive) and behavioural changes at work and home – specific behavioural drills are introduced to be practised in the work environment, e.g. having fewer meetings, scheduling telephone calls, allotting free time periods and so on. (See Cooper and Davidson's book *High Pressure* for more details.) In addition, there is a need for both family and friends to encourage the participant to be involved in the modification programme (Burke, Weir and DuWors, 1979).

Finally, managers, especially women managers, must learn techniques that will help them to relax: transcendental meditation, breathing exercises, yoga, etc. (Cooper and Davidson, 1982). Certainly, relaxation techniques may in the short-term help the individual prepare his/her bodily processes for the stresses and pressures of everyday life.

Each person responds differently to stress in their environment, as the qualitative and quantitative results from this study have demonstrated. It is important for the woman manager to be able to identify accurately those single or series of related incidents that may be causing her stress or tensions.

In summary, based on the overall results of our large-scale study, we recommend the following training measures:

ALL MANAGEMENT COURSES

(1)   *High pressure* associated with *making mistakes, work overload* and *time pressures/deadlines,* along with lack of *consultation/communication* are reported by both men and women managers from supervisors to senior executives. Managers should be taught to cope effectively with their workload pressures, e.g. time and motion exercises; learning to say 'no' to extra work, etc. In addition, their personal and organizational consultation and communication networks and systems, should be investigated and reappraised.

(2)   The *'high risk profiles'* of both male and female managers isolated in this study, should be made known to all managers and personnel officers and utilized constructively as an aid to identifying and helping potentially high risk employees in terms of potential stress-related maladies.

(3)   All management training courses should highlight the potential pressures (both the similarities and the differences) faced by women and men managers at different levels of the management hierarchy. Middle and senior managers in particular, should be made aware that the majority of women in junior and middle management positions still feel *undervalued* and *discriminated against* because of their sex, in relation to future career advancement as well as perform-ance pressure, i.e. having to perform better at their job than other male colleagues. Managers at all levels, should review and endeavour to change the situation of women managers in their own organization.

(4)   Mixed male and female management courses should be *specifically designed* to enable men and women to be aware

of, and able to cope with, the potential problems of working together. Managers should be taught methods of working together in harmony and as *equals*, regardless of gender. We believe that these specialized management courses are *essential in order to promote better understanding, attitude and behavioural changes,* in both male and female managers.

(5) All managers should be taught to find and develop a *relaxation technique* (or techniques) which works for them as an individual. Managers should also be taught techniques to *modify their coronary Type A behaviour.*

MALE MANAGERS ON MANAGEMENT COURSES

(1) Male managers need to be taught to adopt more *efficient,* more *sensitive, sympathetic* and more *cooperative* management styles.

(2) Male manager training needs appear to be orientated towards general business skills with the exception of *male junior managers* who, like their female counterparts, would particularly benefit from interpersonal skills training, including assertion/confidence skills.

(3) Male managers should be taught to *cope effectively with the pressures associated with their leadership/authority role and duties;* they should be given role play exercises involving disciplining subordinates, having to sack someone, etc.

(4) Male supervisors appear to be the most 'high risk' group of either male or female managers, in relation to job dissatisfaction. They complain of very specific job-related pressures: long working hours, staff shortages, equipment failures, unclear career prospects, poor rates of pay and redundancy threats. Clearly they require specially designed training courses. Indeed, male supervisors complain of far more work pressures than any of the other male management categories, and we recommend that their problems receive further attention.

FEMALE MANAGERS ON MANAGEMENT COURSES

(1)   Female managers need to be taught to adopt more *flexible* management styles.

(2)   Like their male counterparts, female managers require general business training skills and female junior managers in particular would benefit from learning how to cope with company politics.

(3)   Women in *junior* and *middle* management would appear to benefit from interpersonal skills training with special emphasis on *assertion/confidence skills training* (a finding confirmed both by the interviews and survey questionnaires). Thus, we believe these results would tend to *support single sex management training for women managers, especially at junior management level,* when emphasis could be made on these specific training skills. However, the problems and barriers facing women managers at work are largely due to inequality of treatment and discrimination/prejudice from organizations and male employees. Therefore, *mixed male and female management courses are also essential,* in order to expose these potential problem areas and remedy them.

Self-help

Finally, we thought that the reader might be interested in some suggestions by top female managers, as to how women can help themselves:

BULLYING: HOW A FEMALE DIRECTOR COPED

'Increasingly I come across executives of both sexes, but predominantly men, who have been so indoctrinated with management 'techniques' that they lose sight of the job in hand. These 'techniques' seem to become more important, more real than the actual project!

    Too many meetings and *far* too many documents are crammed with a confusion of flow charts, critical path analyses, computer projections, decision trees and plenty of other clever tricks. Fine as aids to achieve objectives, but sadly they are often used successfully to camouflage indecisiveness, buck-passing, or a lack of creativity.

My solution is to ask tactfully as soon as possible for a brief explanation in plain English of any suspect gobbledegook. This is unpopular because it is an interruption, but I think it's important because lots of plans get passed simply because no one else dares to admit they are baffled; or, being incomprehensible, such plans are glossed over due to boredom.

I work in a service industry and find that a certain type of male client feels obliged to assert his superiority by bullying or denigrating me, and asking me to undertake tasks he would never *dare* ask of his (or my) male counterparts.

If anyone else suffers this, they could try one of these ploys, but take care to select the more appropriate and get the timing right!

(1)   When a particularly uncalled-for comment is made in public, say so, and calmly ask for it to be withdrawn. Be 100 per cent certain of your facts and choose a major 'bully' or 'squash'. Pettiness is unattractive and tends to be labelled feminine niggling.

(2)   Telephone the offender as soon as is practical after a particularly serious case of bullying has occurred and politely but firmly point out that his approach is hurtful and anti-productive. Explain that you do not like being diminished unfairly in front of colleagues/clients.

'ONE OF THE BOYS': ADVICE FROM A WOMAN MARKETING EXECUTIVE

(1)   Do not fall into the trap of trying to be 'one of the boys'.
(2)   Develop your own style of management and let it evolve as you gain experience.
(3)   Try not to drift – make decisions about your career – do not look at the next step up the ladder simply because it's there – decide if *you* want to be there and the effects it will have on other aspects of your life.
(4)   If female, do not overcompensate by being excessively 'tough' and inflexible. (I know, I've been there!)
(5)   Try not to be excessively conscious that you are a female in a

male-dominated society – once you've got the job you're just another executive expected to perform.

(6)   Be feminine – but do not play on your femaleness.
(7)   Do not bridle when men open doors and offer seats – welcome it and accept it graciously.
(8)   Promote the image that you are a competent executive – not a competent female executive.

CARING AND NOT CARING: WORDS OF WISDOM FROM A MANAGING DIRECTOR

(1)   Remembering that as a manager I go to work to do a job, not to be liked. That is a bonus, when it happens.
(2)   Having very clearly defined personal professional standards and keeping these in focus the whole time.
(3)   Having the ability to be two different people – the work you and the real you. Not seeing this as a source of conflict.
(4)   Being as honest with yourself as you can be.
(5)   Realizing that the world is full of individuals whose level of understanding/perception is very limited, and accepting this.
(6)   Not giving a toss re the jealousy displayed by non-management females on your 'good fortune'.
(7)   Having a sense of humour!
(8)   Being blessed with a boss who sees you for what you are worth.
(9)   Being prepared to take a few risks.
(10)   Accepting that being female in a job can be an advantage – not for the obvious reasons, but because it allows one to act in a catalyst role that would be denied a man.

PUTTING THE MALE CHAUVINISTS AT A DISADVANTAGE: TIPS FROM A PERSONNEL DIRECTOR

Far from feeling that being female in a predominantly male world is a disadvantage, I have found that a clever female can turn this to her advantage. A woman can be efficient yet remain feminine, which puts the male chauvinist at a disadvantage.

Do not try to be the same as men, accept the differences and do not blame sex for failure to succeed. More often than not there will be an entirely different reason.

Do not get too earnest or obsessed with male/female equality and do not take life too seriously.

In the final analysis, one cannot rely solely on legalistic approaches to equal rights, but must hope that individuals, organizations and governments can work together.

Appendix: survey questionnaire

SECTION A

For purposes of statistical analysis *only*, please answer the following questions about yourself. Your answers will remain *anonymous and strictly confidential*. However, this biographical data is *crucial* to the study.

Answer the following questions by *circling* the most appropriate response unless otherwise instructed.

1. What is your job title? _____

2. Would you describe yourself as a:

   Supervisor   1
   Junior Manager   2
   Middle Manager   3
   Senior Manager   4

3. Are you the first person to hold this job title?

   Yes   1
   No   2

4. Are you the first person of your sex to hold this job title?

   Yes   1
   No   2

5. What is your age?

   Under 25   1
   26–30   2
   31–35   3
   36–40   4
   41–50   5
   51–60   6
   Over 60   7

6. What is your sex?

   Female   1
   Male   2

7. Are you:

   Married   1
   Remarried   2
   Living together   3
   Single   4
   Divorced/Separated   5
   Widow/Widower   6

8. Number of children:

None	1
One	2
Two	3
Three	4
Four or more	5

9. Age of children:

Not applicable	1
All pre-school age	2
Pre-school age and school age	3
All school age	4
School age and post school age	5
All post school age	6

10. Do you have other dependants (besides children) living at home with you?

Yes	1
No	2

11. What is the highest educational qualification, if any, you have attained?

None	1
GCE 'O' Level/CSE	2
'A' Level/Ordinary National Diploma	3
Higher National Diploma or equivalent	4
University Degree	5
MA/MSc	6
PhD	7
Other (please specify)	
_____	8

12. Do you have additional professional qualifications?

Yes	1	Please specify _____
No	2	_____

13. How many years have you been in full-time employment in your present job?

_____

14. How many years have you been a full-time employee for the company/organisation you presently work for?

_____

15. What is the total number of years over your entire lifetime during which you have been a full-time employee?

_____

16. What is the total number of companies/organisations you have worked for?

_____

17. Have you worked as a full-time employee continuously without leaving the workforce?

Yes	1
No	2

18. If you answered *No* to question 17:
    (a) Have you ever worked part-time?
       Yes   1
       No   2
    (b) How many years was your break from the workforce?

---

19. What is your annual salary?

Under £4,000	01
£4,000–£6,000	02
£6,000–£8,000	03
£8,000–£10,000	04
£10,000–£12,000	05
£12,000–£14,000	06
£14,000–£16,000	07
£16,000–£18,000	08
£18,000–£20,000	09
Over £20,000	10

20. How many people do you supervise (i.e. how many people *in total* are directly and indirectly under your *management*)?

---

21. Are your colleagues/peers at work:

All female	1
Both male and female	2
Have no colleagues	3
All male	4

22. What are the total number of employees in your company/organization?

Up to 200	1
200–500	2
500–1,000	3
Over 1,000	4

23. Does your company/organization constitute:

Predominantly women at all levels of the hierarchy	1
About 50% women and 50% men at all levels of the hierarchy	2
Predominantly women, with predominantly men in senior management	3
About 50% women and 50% men, with predominantly women in senior management	4
About 50% women and 50% men, with predominantly men in senior management	5
Predominantly men at all levels of the hierarchy	6

SECTION B

Could you please circle the number that best reflects the degree to which the particular statement is a source of pressure at work.

Only when a statement/situation *does not apply to you,* circle NA for Not Applicable, e.g. circle NA for *'shiftwork'* if you do not have shiftwork working hours, or circle NA for *'Sacking Someone'* if your job never requires you to sack someone.

Remember do not spend time pondering, there are no right or wrong answers. You will find completion of this questionnaire easiest if you do it fairly swiftly.

Definitions
Pressure: is defined as a problem, something you find difficult to cope with, about which you feel worried or anxious.

Codes: 5 = a source of *extreme* pressure
3 = a source of *moderate* pressure
1 = no pressure at all

Therefore if *work overload* is a *slight* pressure for you, you would circle ②, e.g.

	No pressure at all				A great deal of pressure	
Work overload	1	②	3	4	5	NA

Or, if *Lack of support from superiors* is not a problem for you, and is *no pressure at all* for you, you would circle ①, e.g.

Lack of support from superiors	①	2	3	4	5	NA

		No pressure at all				A great deal of pressure	
1	Work overload	1	2	3	4	5	NA
2	Work underload	1	2	3	4	5	NA
3	Time pressures and deadlines	1	2	3	4	5	NA
4	Overpromotion – promoted beyond my competence	1	2	3	4	5	NA
5	Underpromotion – employed beneath my competence	1	2	3	4	5	NA
6	Rate of pay	1	2	3	4	5	NA
7	The amount of travel required by my work	1	2	3	4	5	NA
8	Taking my work home	1	2	3	4	5	NA
9	Managing/supervising people	1	2	3	4	5	NA
10	Lack of control in my work environment	1	2	3	4	5	NA
11	Office politics	1	2	3	4	5	NA
12	Lack of power and influence	1	2	3	4	5	NA
13	My beliefs conflicting with those of the company/organisation	1	2	3	4	5	NA
14	Lack of consultation and communication	1	2	3	4	5	NA
15	Clarity of my job role/job duties	1	2	3	4	5	NA
16	Inadequate supervision	1	2	3	4	5	NA
17	Lack of support from superiors	1	2	3	4	5	NA

		No pressure at all					A great deal of pressure
18	Staff shortages and staff turnover rates	1	2	3	4	5	NA
19	Conflicting job demands, loyalties, etc	1	2	3	4	5	NA
20	Disciplining subordinates	1	2	3	4	5	NA
21	Sacking someone	1	2	3	4	5	NA
22	Inadequate feedback on my work	1	2	3	4	5	NA
23	Inability to delegate	1	2	3	4	5	NA
24	Poor work environment	1	2	3	4	5	NA
25	Lack of social support from people at work	1	2	3	4	5	NA
26	Lack of encouragement from superiors	1	2	3	4	5	NA
27	Keeping up with new technology/equipment	1	2	3	4	5	NA
28	Inadequate resources and finances	1	2	3	4	5	NA
29	Sex discrimination and prejudice	1	2	3	4	5	NA
30	Inadequate job and training experience compared to colleagues of the opposite sex	1	2	3	4	5	NA
31	Colleagues of the opposite sex being treated more favourably by management	1	2	3	4	5	NA
32	Attending meetings	1	2	3	4	5	NA
33	Shift work	1	2	3	4	5	NA
34	New challenges and risk	1	2	3	4	5	NA
35	Redundancy threat	1	2	3	4	5	NA
36	Long working hours	1	2	3	4	5	NA
37	Equipment failures	1	2	3	4	5	NA
38	Too much responsibility	1	2	3	4	5	NA
39	Administration and paperwork	1	2	3	4	5	NA
40	Having to move with my job in order to progress in my career	1	2	3	4	5	NA
41	Not being able to move with my job in order to progress in my career	1	2	3	4	5	NA
42	Having to stand on my feet all day	1	2	3	4	5	NA
43	Being 'the boss'	1	2	3	4	5	NA
44	Unclear progress prospects	1	2	3	4	5	NA
45	Sexual harassment of a verbal or physical nature	1	2	3	4	5	NA
46	Being visible	1	2	3	4	5	NA
47	Feeling isolated	1	2	3	4	5	NA
48	Feeling undervalued	1	2	3	4	5	NA
49	Lack of variety at work	1	2	3	4	5	NA

		No pressure at all					A great deal of pressure	
50	Playing the counsellor role at work	1	2	3	4	5	NA
51	Working relationships with male superiors	1	2	3	4	5	NA
52	Working relationships with male colleagues/peers	1	2	3	4	5	NA
53	Working relationships with male subordinates	1	2	3	4	5	NA
54	Working relationships with female superiors	1	2	3	4	5	NA
55	Working relationships with female colleagues/peers	1	2	3	4	5	NA
56	Working relationships with female subordinates	1	2	3	4	5	NA
57	Lack of same sex role models – person of the same sex in a position above me, acting as an example	1	2	3	4	5	NA
58	Members of the opposite sex seem uncomfortable working with me because of my sex	1	2	3	4	5	NA
59	I feel uncomfortable working with members of the opposite sex	1	2	3	4	5	NA
60	I feel my sex is a disadvantage when it comes to job promotion/career progress prospects	1	2	3	4	5	NA
61	Members of the opposite sex at work try and force me into behaviours they associate with my sex, rather than letting me 'be myself'	1	2	3	4	5	NA
62	Feeling I have to perform better at my job than colleagues of the opposite sex	1	2	3	4	5	NA
63	Experiencing prejudiced attitudes from members of the opposite sex at work because of my sex	1	2	3	4	5	NA
64	Experiencing prejudiced attitudes from members of the same sex at work because of my sex	1	2	3	4	5	NA
65	I feel uncomfortable on training courses when a member of the minority sex	1	2	3	4	5	NA
66	My spouse/partner's attitude towards my career	1	2	3	4	5	NA

	No pressure at all				A great deal of pressure	
67 Demands of work on my relationship with my children	1	2	3	4	5	NA
68 Demands of work on my relationship with spouse/partner	1	2	3	4	5	NA
69 Earning more than my spouse/partner	1	2	3	4	5	NA
70 Dependants (other than children) living at home	1	2	3	4	5	NA
71 My career related dilemma concerning whether to marry/live with someone	1	2	3	4	5	NA
72 My career related dilemma concerning whether to start a family	1	2	3	4	5	NA
73 Being single, other people sometimes label me as a bit of an 'oddity'	1	2	3	4	5	NA
74 Being single I am sometimes excluded from social and business events such as dinner parties	1	2	3	4	5	NA
75 Business travel and staying in hotels alone	1	2	3	4	5	NA
76 Lack of emotional support at home	1	2	3	4	5	NA
77 Lack of domestic support at home	1	2	3	4	5	NA
78 Demands of work on my private/social life	1	2	3	4	5	NA
79 Conflicting responsibilities associated with running a home and career	1	2	3	4	5	NA
80 Other (please state)						

_____

_____

SECTION C

Below is a list of different troubles and complaints which people often have. Please circle the number which best reflects how often you have felt like this during the last *three months*.

I feel like this:

		Never	Rarely	Sometimes	Often	Always
1	Do you ever have any trouble getting to sleep or staying asleep?	1	2	3	4	5
2	Have you ever been bothered by nervousness, feeling fidgety or tense?	1	2	3	4	5
3	Are you ever troubled by headaches or pains in the head?	1	2	3	4	5
4	Are there any times when you just don't feel like eating?	1	2	3	4	5
5	Are there times when you get tired very easily?	1	2	3	4	5
6	How often are you bothered by having an upset stomach?	1	2	3	4	5
7	Do you find it difficult to get up in the morning?	1	2	3	4	5
8	Does ill-health ever affect the amount of work you do?	1	2	3	4	5
9	Are you ever bothered by shortness of breath when you are not exercising or working hard?	1	2	3	4	5
10	Do you ever feel 'put out' if something unexpected happens?	1	2	3	4	5
11	Are there times when you tend to cry easily?	1	2	3	4	5
12	Have you ever been bothered by your heart beating hard?	1	2	3	4	5
13	Do you ever smoke, drink, or eat more than you should?	1	2	3	4	5
14	Do you ever have spells of dizziness?	1	2	3	4	5
15	Are you ever bothered by nightmares?	1	2	3	4	5
16	Do your muscles ever tremble enough to bother you (e.g. hands tremble, eyes twitch)?	1	2	3	4	5
17	Do you ever feel mentally exhausted and have difficulty in concentrating or thinking clearly?	1	2	3	4	5

I feel like this:

	Never	Rarely	Sometimes	Often	Always
18 Are you troubled by your hands sweating so that you feel damp and clammy?	1	2	3	4	5
19 Have there ever been times when you couldn't take care of things because you just couldn't get going?	1	2	3	4	5
20 Do you ever just want to be left alone?	1	2	3	4	5

TO THE REMAINING QUESTIONS PLEASE ANSWER
'YES' OR 'NO'

	No	Yes
21 Do you feel you are bothered by all sorts of pains and ailments in different parts of your body?	1	2
22 For the most part do you feel healthy enough to carry out the things you would like to do?	1	2
23 Have you ever felt that you were going to have a nervous breakdown?	1	2
24 Do you have any particular physical or health problem?	1	2

SECTION D

I   How often do you use the following measures to relax?

	Never	Rarely	Sometimes	Often	Always
1 Take aspirin	1	2	3	4	5
2 Use tranquillizers or other medication	1	2	3	4	5
3 Drink coffee, Coke or eat frequently	1	2	3	4	5
4 Smoke	1	2	3	4	5
5 Have an alcoholic drink	1	2	3	4	5
6 Use relaxation techniques (meditation, yoga)	1	2	3	4	5
7 Use informal relaxation techniques (i.e. take time out for deep breathing, imagining pleasant scenes)	1	2	3	4	5
8 Exercise	1	2	3	4	5
9 Talk to someone you know	1	2	3	4	5

		Never	Rarely	Sometimes	Often	Always
10	Leave your work area and go somewhere (time out, sick days, lunch away from organisation etc)	1	2	3	4	5
11	Use humour	1	2	3	4	5
12	Other_____	1	2	3	4	5

II   Over the past year, which of the following best describes your typical drinking habits? (one drink is a single whisky, gin or brandy; a glass of wine, sherry or port; or ½ pint of beer)

Teetotal	1
An occasional drink	2
Several drinks a week, but not every day	3
Regularly, 1 or 2 drinks a day	4
Regularly, 3–6 drinks a day	5
Regularly more than 6 drinks a day	6

III   Re: cigarette smoking. Which of the following statements is most nearly true for you?

I have never smoked regularly	1
I have given up smoking	2
I am currently smoking	3

IV   If you are currently smoking, please circle the number which constitutes your average daily consumption of cigarettes:

0–5 a day	1
5–10 a day	2
10–15 a day	3
15–20 a day	4
20–30 a day	5
30–40 a day	6
40 plus a day	7

V   Please circle the number which best describes how you feel about your present job.

	Strongly agree	Agree	Undecided	Disagree	Strongly disagree
I feel fairly well satisfied with my present job	1	2	3	4	5
I find real enjoyment in my work	1	2	3	4	5

VI How often do you adopt the following
    management/supervisory styles at work?

	Never	Rarely	Sometimes	Often	Always
Flexible	1	2	3	4	5
Efficient	1	2	3	4	5
Directive	1	2	3	4	5
Authoritative	1	2	3	4	5
Positive	1	2	3	4	5
Sensitive, sympathetic	1	2	3	4	5
Consultative, e.g. joint problem solving	1	2	3	4	5
Cooperative	1	2	3	4	5
Assertive	1	2	3	4	5
Dogmatic	1	2	3	4	5

VII How often do you feel the following at work?:

		Never	Rarely	Sometimes	Often	Always
1	Unable to use my skills and knowledge	1	2	3	4	5
2	Unable to make decisions	1	2	3	4	5
3	Unable to meet deadlines	1	2	3	4	5
4	Unable to produce a satisfactory quantity of work	1	2	3	4	5
5	Unable to produce a satisfactory quality of work	1	2	3	4	5
6	Unable to manage/supervise people satisfactorily	1	2	3	4	5
7	Lack confidence in putting forward my point of view (e.g. at meetings)	1	2	3	4	5
8	Unable to be successful	1	2	3	4	5
9	Unable to do my best	1	2	3	4	5
10	Unable to plan and organise work	1	2	3	4	5
11	Unable to influence and persuade people	1	2	3	4	5
12	Unable to 'sell myself' in competitive situations (inadequate self-presentation)	1	2	3	4	5
13	Unable to cope well in conflict situations	1	2	3	4	5
14	Reacting too emotionally when faced with problems	1	2	3	4	5
15	Making mistakes	1	2	3	4	5
16	Lack of self-confidence in the ability to do my job	1	2	3	4	5

VIII   Could you please circle the *one* number which you feel most closely represents your own behaviour?

Never late	5	4	3	2	1	0	1	2	3	4	5	Casual about appointments
Anticipates what others are going to say (nods, interrupts, finishes for them)	5	4	3	2	1	0	1	2	3	4	5	Good listener
Always rushed	5	4	3	2	1	0	1	2	3	4	5	Never feels rushed (even under pressure)
Can wait patiently	5	4	3	2	1	0	1	2	3	4	5	Impatient whilst waiting
Goes all out	5	4	3	2	1	0	1	2	3	4	5	Casual
Takes things one at a time	5	4	3	2	1	0	1	2	3	4	5	Tries to do many things at once, thinks what he/she is about to do next
Emphatic in speech (may pound desk)	5	4	3	2	1	0	1	2	3	4	5	Slow, deliberate talker
Wants good job recognised by others	5	4	3	2	1	0	1	2	3	4	5	Cares about satisfying him/herself no matter what others think
Fast (eating, working, etc)	5	4	3	2	1	0	1	2	3	4	5	Slow doing things
Easy going	5	4	3	2	1	0	1	2	3	4	5	Hard driving
Hides feelings	5	4	3	2	1	0	1	2	3	4	5	Expresses feelings
Many outside interests	5	4	3	2	1	0	1	2	3	4	5	Few interests outside work

SECTION E

Thank you for completing this questionnaire. Please write below any other comments you may wish to add, e.g. experiences/techniques you have personally found useful in coping with the problems and pressures associated with being in management/supervision.

Bibliography

Alberti, R. E. & Emmons, M. L. (1970), *Your Perfect Right: A Guide to Assertive Behaviour*, London: Impact.

Bartol, K. M. (1980), 'Female managers and quality of working life: the impact of sex-role stereotypes', *Journal of Occupational Behaviour*, 1, 205–221.

Berk, R. A. & Berk, S. F. (1978) 'A simultaneous equation model for the division of household labor', *Sociological Methods and Research*, 6, 431–68.

Berne, E. (1964), *Games People Play*, New York: Grove Press.

Bhagat, R. S. & Chassie, M. B. (1981), 'Determinants of organisational commitment in working women: some implications for organisational integration', *Journal of Occupational Behaviour*, 2, 2, 17–30.

Birnbaum, J. A. (1975), 'Life patterns and self-esteem in gifted family-orientated and career-committed women', in *Women and Achievement*, Mednick, M. T. S., Tangri, S. S. & Offman, L. W. (eds), Washington DC: Hemispheric Publishing.

Blackstone, T. & Weinreich-Haste, H. (1980), 'Why are there so few women scientists and engineers?', *New Society*, 51, 383–5.

Bortner, R. W. & Rosenman, R. H. (1967), 'The measurement of pattern: a behaviour', *Journal of Chronic Disease*, 20, 525–33.

Braun, L. K. (1982), *The Woman Manager in the United States*, Washington: Business & Professional Women's Foundation Press.

Burke, R. J. & Deszca, E. (1982), 'Preferred organisational climates of Type A individuals', *Journal of Vocational Behaviour*, 21, 50–9.

Burke, R. J., & Deszca E. (1982), 'Career success and personal failure experience and Type A behaviour', *Journal of Occupational Behaviour*, 3, 161–170.

Burke, R. J., Weir, T., & Duwors, R. E. (1979), 'Type A behaviour of administrators and wives' reports of marital satisfaction and well-being', *Journal of Applied Psychology*, 64, 57–65.

Cairncross, F. (1982), 'How marriage went out of fashion: the fading family', *The Guardian*, 25 May 1982.

Caplan, R. D., Cobb, S., & French, J. R. P. (1975), *Job Demands and Workers Health*, Washington DC: US Department of Health, Education and Welfare Publication no. (NIOSH) 75–160. US Government Printing Office.

Carruthers, M. (1980), 'Hazardous occupations and the heart', in *Current Concerns in Occupational Stress,* Cooper, C. L. & Payne, R. (eds). Chichester, New York: John Wiley & Sons, 3–22.

Caulkin, S. (1977), 'Women in management'. *Management Today,* Sept., 1977, 58–63.

Chacko, T. I. (1982), 'Women and equal employment opportunity: some unintended effects', *Journal of Applied Psychology,* **62**, 1, 119–23.

Chesney, M. A. & Rosenman, R. H. (1980), 'Type A behaviour in the work setting', in *Current Concerns in Occupational Stress,* Cooper, C. L. & Payne, R. (eds), London: John Wiley & Sons.

Cherlin, A. (1982), *Marriage, Divorce, Remarriage,* Boston: Harvard, University Press.

Cherry, N. (1978), 'Stress, anxiety and work', *Journal of Occupational Psychology,* **51**, 259–70.

Child, D. (1970), *The Essentials of Factor Analysis,* London: Holt, Rinehart & Winston.

Collins, E. G. C. & Blodgett, T. B. (1981), 'Sexual harassment – some see it, some won't', *Harvard Business Review,* **59**, 2, 76–95.

Collins, J. W. & Gantis, C. G. (1974), 'Managerial attitudes toward corporate social responsibility', in Sethi, S. P. (ed.) *The Unstable Ground: Corporate Social Policy in a Dynamic Society,* Los Angeles: Melville Publishing.

Cooper, C. L. (1980a), 'Coronaries: the risks to working women', *The Times,* Dec. 1980.

Cooper, C. L. (1980b), 'Work stress in white and blue collar jobs', *Bulletin of the British Psychological Society,* **33**, 49–51.

Cooper, C. L. (1981), *The Stress Check,* Englewood Cliffs, New Jersey: Prentice–Hall.

Cooper, C. L. (1982), *Executive Families Under Stress,* New Jersey: Prentice–Hall.

Cooper, C. L. & Davidson, M. J. (1981), 'The Pressures of working women: what can be done?', *Bulletin of the British Psychological Society,* **34**, 357–60.

Cooper, C. L. & Davidson, M. J. (1982), *High Pressure – Working Lives of Women Managers,* London: Fontana.

Cooper, C. L. & Lewis, B. (1979), 'The femanager boom', *Management Today,* July, 46–7.

Cooper, C. L. & Marshall, J. (1976), 'Occupational sources of stress: a review of the literature relating to coronary heart disease and mental ill-health', *Journal of Occupational Psychology,* **49**, 11–28.

Cooper, C. L. & Marshall, J. (1978), *Understanding Executive Stress,* London: Macmillan.

Cooper, C. L. & Melhuish, A. (1980), 'Occupational stress and managers', *Journal of Occupational Medicine,* **22**, 9, 588–92.

Cooper, C. L. & Payne, R. (eds) (1980), *Current Concerns in Occupational Stress,* Chichester: John Wiley & Sons.

Cox, T. (1980), 'Repetitive work', in *Current Concerns in Occupational Stress*, Cooper, C. L. & Payne, R. (eds), Chichester, New York: John Wiley & Sons, 23–42.

Crow, G. (1981), 'Whither the mistresses of business administration?', *Personnel Management*, Sept., 36–9.

Davidson, M. J. & Cooper, C. L. (1980a), 'The extra pressures on women executives', *Personnel Management*, **12**, 6, 48–51.

Davidson, M. J. & Cooper, C. L. (1980b), 'Type A coronary-prone behaviour and stress in senior female managers and administrators', *Journal of Occupational Medicine*, **22**, (12), 801–5.

Davidson, M. J. & Cooper, C. L. (1981a), 'The token woman enmeshed in the old boy network'. *The Guardian*, 4 Aug. 1981.

Davidson, M. J. & Cooper, C. L. (1981b), 'A model of occupational stress', *Journal of Occupational Medicine*, **23**, 8, 564–74.

Davidson, M. J. & Cooper, C. L. (1981c), 'Type A coronary-prone behaviour in the work environment', *Journal of Occupational Medicine*, **22**, 6, 375–83.

Davidson, M. J. & Veno, A. (1980), 'Stress and the policeman', in *White Collar and Professional Stress*, Cooper, C. L. & Marshall, J. (eds), London: John Wiley & Sons.

Denmarke, F. L. & Diggory, J. C. (1976), 'Sex differences in attitudes toward leader's display of authoritarian behaviour', *Psychological Reports*, **18**, 12–16.

Department of Employment, (1979), *Equal Pay and Opportunities*, Research Paper No. 10, London: Department of Employment.

Dipboye, R. L. (1978), 'Women as managers', in *Women in Management*, Stead, B. A. (ed.), Prentice–Hall Inc. Englewood Cliffs: New Jersey.

EEC Labour Force Survey (1979) London: HMSO.

Equal Opportunities Commission (1981), *Fifth Annual Report, 1980*, Manchester: EOC.

Ezell, H. F., Odewahn, C. A. & Sherman, J. D. (1981), 'The effects of having been supervised by a woman on perceptions of female managerial competence', *Personnel Psychology*, **34**, 2, 291–9.

Farley, L. (1980), *Sexual Shakedown*, New York: Warner Brooks, McGraw–Hill.

Finn, F. Hickley, N., & O'Doherty, E. F. (1969), 'The psychological profiles of male and female patients with CHD', *Irish Journal of Medical Science*, **2**, 339–41.

Frankenhaeuser, M. (1974), *Man in Technological Society: Stress, Adaptation and Tolerance Limits*, reports from the psychological laboratories, The University of Stockholm, Supplement 26.

Frankenhaeuser, M., Lunberg, U., & Forsman, L. (1980), 'Note on arousing Type A persons by depriving them of work', *Journal of Psychosomatic Research*, **24**, 45–7.

French, J. R. P. & Caplan, R. D. (1970), 'Psychosocial factors in coronary heart disease, *Industrial Medicine*, **39**, 383–97.

French, J. R. P. & Caplan, R. (1972), 'Organisational stress and individual strain', in *The Failure of Success,* Marrow, A. J. (ed.), New York: Amacon.

Friedman, M., Rosenman, R. H. (1974), *Type A Behaviour and Your Heart,* London: Wildwood House.

Fritchie, R. (1981), *Women into Management,* Development Digest, No. 5 (Gloucester: Food, Drink and Tobacco Industry Training Board).

Garrity, T. F. Somes, G. W., & Marx, M. B. (1977). 'Personality factors in resistance to illness after recent life changes'. *Journal of Psychosomatic Research,* **21**, 23–32.

General Household Survey (1980), London: HMSO.

General Household Survey (1981), London: HMSO.

Gurin, G., Veroff, J., and Feld, S. (1960), *American's View their Mental Health.* New York: Basic Books.

Gutek, B., Nakamura, C. U., & Nieva, V. G. (1981), 'The interdependence of work and family roles', *Journal of Occupational Behaviour,* **2**, 1, 1–16.

Hakim, C. (1979), 'Occupational segregation', Research Paper No. 9. London: Department of Employment.

Hakim, C. (1981), 'The rise of the working woman: a twentieth century myth', Paper presented at the British Association, York.

Hall, D. T. (1972), 'A model of coping with role conflict. The role behaviour of college educated women', *Administrative Science Quarterly,* **17**, 471–86.

Hall, F. S. & Hall, D. T. (1978), 'Dual careers – how do couples and companies cope with the problem?', *Organisational Dynamics,* **6**, 4, 57–77.

Hall, D. F. & Hall, F. (1980), 'Stress and the two career couple', in C. L. Cooper and R. Payne (eds), *Current Concerns in Occupational Stress,* London: John Wiley & Sons.

Hammerton, M. & Tickner, A. H. (1968), 'An investigation into the effects of stress upon skilled performance', *Ergonomics,* **12**, 851–5.

Harlan, A. & Weiss, C. (1980), *Moving Up: Women in Managerial Careers: Third Progress Report,* Welsley, Mass: Welsley Centre for Research on Women.

Harnett, O. & Novarra, V. (1979), 'Facilitating the entry of women into management posts'. Paper presented at Association of Teachers of Management Conference, The Training and Development Needs of Women Managers. London, November.

Harnett, O. & Novarra, V. (1980), 'Single sex management training and a woman's touch', *Personnel Management,* **12**, 3, 32–5.

Haynes, S. G. & Feinleib, M. (1980), 'Women, work and coronary heart disease: prospective findings from the Framingham Heart Study', *American Journal of Public Health,* **70**, 133–41.

Hennig, M. & Jardim, A. (1979), *The Managerial Woman,* London: Pan Books.

Herbert, S. G. & Yost, E. B.L (1979), 'Women as effective managers: a strategic model for overcoming the barriers', *Human Resources Management*, **17**, 18–25.

Hinkle, L. E. (1973). 'The concept of "stress" in the biological and social sciences', *Science, Medicine and Man*, **1**, 31–48.

Horner, K. (1970)., 'Femininity and successful achievement: a basic inconsistency', *Feminine Personality and Conflict*, California: Brooks/Cole.

Howard, J. H., Cunningham, D. A, & Rechnitzer, P. A. (1976), 'Health patterns associated with Type A behaviour: a managerial population', *Journal of Human Stress*, **2**, 24–31.

Hoyland, P. (1980), 'Alcoholism affects one person in twenty-five', *The Guardian*, June 1980.

Hunt, A. (1975), *OPCS: Survey of Management Attitudes and Practices Towards Women at Work*, HMSO.

Ikard, P. F. & Tomkins, S. (1973), 'The experience of affect as a determinant of smoking behaviour', *Journal of Abnormal Psychology*, **81**, 172–81.

ILO Yearbook of Labour Statistics, (1979), Geneva.

Industrial Society, (1980), *Women in Management – Onwards and Upwards?*, London: Industrial Society.

Izraeli, D. N., Banai, M., & Zeira, Y. (1980), 'Women executives in MNC (Multinational Corporations) subsidiaries', *California Management Review*, **1**, XXIII, 53–63.

Jacobson, B. (1981), *The Ladykillers: Why Smoking is a Feminist Issue*, Pluto Press: London.

Jenkins, C. D. (1971), 'Psychologic and social precursors of coronary diseases', *New England Journal of Medicine*, **284**, 5, 244–255.

Kanter, R. (1977), *Men and Women of the Corporation*, New York: Basic Books.

Kasl, S. V. (1973), 'Mental health and work environment: an examination of the evidence', *Journal of Occupational Medicine*, **15**, 506–15.

Kasl, S. V. (1978), 'Epidemiological contributions to the study of work stress', in *Stress at Work*, Cooper, C. L. & Payne, R. (eds), Chichester, New York: John Wiley & Sons.

Kavanagh, J. J. & Halpern, M. (1977), 'The impact of job level and sex differences on the relationship between life and job satisfaction', *Academy of Management Journal*, **20**, 66–73.

Kennedy, A. C. (1978), 'Acute poisoning', in *A Textbook of Medical Treatment*, Alstead, S. & Girdwood, R. H. (eds), London: Churchill Livngston.

Kenny, M. (1979), *Women × Two – How to Cope with a Double Life*, Feltham: Hamlyn Paperbacks.

Lamb, R. W. (1981) 'Feminism: the revised version', *The Sunday Times Magazine*, 15 Nov. 1981, 32–47.

Lancet (1980), Editorial: 'Women, work and coronary heart disease', 12 July, 76–7.

Langrish, S. (1980), 'Single sex management training – a personal view', *Women and Training News*, **1**, Winter, 3–4.

Langrish, S. (1981), 'Why don't women progress to management jobs?', *The Business Graduate*, XI, Spring, 12–13.

Larwood, L. & Kaplan, M. (1980), 'Job tactics of women in banking', *Group and Organisation Studies*, **5**, 1, Mar., 70–9.

Larwood, L. & Lockheed, M. (1979), 'Women as managers: toward second generation research', *Sex Roles*, **5**, 659–66.

Larwood, L. & Wood, M. M. (1977, 1979), *Women in Management*, London: Lexington Books.

Lazarus, R. S. (1966), *Psychological Stress and the Coping Process*, New York: McGraw–Hill.

Levi, L. (1971), *Society, Stress and Disease. The Psychological Environment and Psychosomatic Disease* (VL), London, New York: Oxford University Press.

Litterer, J. A. (1976), 'Life cycle changes of career women: assessment and adaptation', Paper presented at a meeting of the Academy of Management, Kansas City.

Lockwood, B. (1981), 'Equal opportunities for women in management', *The Business Graduate*, **1**, Spring, 3–4.

Margolis, B., Kroes, W. & Quinn, R. (1974), 'Job stress: an unlisted occupational hazard', *Journal of Occupational Medicine*, **1**, 659–61.

Marshall, J. & Cooper, C. L. (1979), *Executives Under Pressure*, London: Macmillan.

McClelland, D. C. (1975), *Power – The Inner Experience*, New York: Irvington Publishing.

McCrae, R. R., Costa, P. T., & Bosse, R. (1978), 'Anxiety, extroversion and smoking', *British Journal of Social and Clinical Psychology*, **17**, 269–73.

McMichael, A. J. (1978), 'Personality, behavioural and situational modifiers of work stressors', in *Stress at Work*, Cooper, C. L. & Payne, R. (eds), Chichester: John Wiley & Sons.

McRae, H. (1980), 'Why British women deserve a seat on the board', *The Guardian*, 8 Aug. 1980.

Miller, J., Labovitz, S. & Fry, L. (1975), 'Inequities in the organisational experience of women and men', *Social Forces*, **54**, 365–81.

Miller, J. B. (1976), *Towards a New Psychology of Woman*, Boston: Beacon Press.

Moore, L. M. & Rickel, A. (1980), 'Characteristics of women in traditional and non-traditional managerial roles', *Personnel Psychology*, **3**, 2, 317–33.

Myers, J. K., Lindenthal, J., Pepper, M.P., & Ostrander, D. R. (1972), 'Life events and mental status: a longitudinal study', *Journal of Health and Social Behaviour*, **13**, 398–406.

National Council for Civil Liberties (1982), *Sexual Harassment at Work*, London: NCCL.

Newberry, P., Weissman, M., & Myers, J. (1979), 'Working wives and housewives: do they differ in mental status and social adjustment?', *American Journal of Orthopsychiatry*, **49**, 282–91.

Novarra, V. (1980), *Women's Work, Men's Work*. London: Marian Boyers.

Novarra, V. (1981), 'Women in management – training for women and training for effective equal opportunity', *The Training Officer*, 10–11.

Oakley, A. (1974), *The Sociology of Housework*, Bath: Martin Robertson.

Oakley, A. (1980), 'For love or money – the unspoken deal', *New Society*, Dec., 3–4.

Otway, H. J. & Misenta, R. (1980), 'The determinants of operator preparedness for emergency situations in nuclear power plants', Paper presented at Workshop on Procedural and Organisational Measures for Accident Management: Laxenburg, Austria, 28–31 Jan.

Paddison, L. (1981), 'Staying power, women in management: note to accompany session at 14th annual occupational psychology conference', University of York, 7–10 Jan.

Petty, M. M. & Bruning, N. S. (1980), 'A comparison of the relationships between subordinates, perceptions of supervisory behaviour and measures of subordinates' job satisfaction for male and female leaders', *Academy of Management Journal*, **23**, 4, 717–25.

Pleck, J. H. (1977), 'The work-family role system', *Social Problems*, **24**, 417–27.

Population Trends, (1982), London: HMSO.

Ramprakash, D. (ed.) (1981), *Social Trends*, No. 11, London: HMSO.

Rapoport, R. & Rapoport, R. (1976), *Dual Career Families Re-examined*, London: Martin Robertson.

Reed, C. (1982), 'Meanwhile, there are American women who are achieving considerable success at work', *The Guardian*, 23 June, 1982.

Reid, I. & Wormald, E. (eds) (1982), *Sex Differences in Britain*, London: Grant McIntyre.

Report on the Census of Production, 1974/75, (1979), PA1002, London: HMSO.

Richbell, S. (1976), 'Defacto discrimination and how to kick the habit', *Personnel Management*, Nov., 30–3.

Ritzer, G. (1977), *Working: Conflict and Change*, New Jersey: Prentice–Hall.

Robarts, S., Coote, A., & Ball, E. (1981), *Positive Action for Women – The Next Stop*, Nottingham: NCCL.

Robson, C. (1973), *Experiment, Design and Statistics in Psychology*, Harmondsworth: Penguin.

Rosenman, R. H. (1978), 'The interview method of assessment of the coronary-prone behaviour pattern', in *Coronary-Prone Behaviour*, Dembroski, Weiss, Shields, *et al.* (eds), New York: Springer–Verlag, 55–69.

Rosenman, R. H. Friedman, M., & Straus, R. (1964), 'A predictive study of CHD', *JAMA,* **189,** 15–22.

Rosenman, R. H., Brand, R. J., Sholtz, R. I., & Friedman, M. (1976), 'Multivariate prediction of coronary heart disease during 8.5 follow-up in the Western collaborative study', *American Journal of Cardiology,* **37,** 903–8.

Rosenman, R. H., Friedman, M., & Straus, R. (1966), 'CHD in the Western collaborative group study', *Journal of the American Medical Association,* **195,** 86–92.

Rosenman, R. H., Friedman, M. & Jenkins, C. D. (1967), 'Clinically unrecognised myocardial infarction in the Western collaborative group study', *American Journal of Cardiology,* **19,** 776–82.

Rosenman, R. H., Jenkins, C. D., Brand, R. J. *et al.* (1975), 'Coronary heart disease in the Western collaborative group study: final follow-up experience of 8.5 years, *JAMA,* **233,** 872–7.

Sadler, P. J. (1970), 'Leadership style, confidence in management and job satisfaction', *The Journal of Applied Behavioural Science,* **6,** 1–8.

Sargent, M. (1973), *Alcoholism as a Social Problem,* St Lucia: University of Queensland Press.

Schein, V. E. (1975), 'The relationship between sex roles stereotypes and requisite management characteristics among female managers', *Journal of Applied Psychology,* **60,** 44–8.

Schuckit, M. A., & Gunderson, E. (1973), 'Job stress and psychiatric illness in the US Navy, *Journal of Occupational Medicine,* **15,** 884–7.

Selye, H. (1976), *Stress in Health and Disease,* London: Butterworth.

Social Trends (1981), London: HMSO.

Social Trends (1981), 'Women in the labour force', *New Society,* 20 Aug., 310.

Spender, D. (1980), 'Man-made language', London: Routledge & Kegan-Paul, 1980.

Spender, D. (1982), *Invisible Women: The Schooling Scandal,* London: Writers and Readers.

Staines, G. L., Pleck, L., Shepard, P. & O'Connor, P. (1979), *Wives Employment Status and Marital Adjustment,* unpublished manuscript, Institute of Social Research, University of Michigan.

Staines, G., Tavris, C., & Hayaratne, T. E. (1973), 'The Queen Bee syndrome', in Tavris, C. (ed.), *The Female Experience,* De Mar, California: CRM Books.

Stead, B. A. (1978), *Women in Management,* Englewood Cliffs, New Jersey: Prentice-Hall Inc.

Steinmetz, J. (1979) Conflict/Stress Questionnaire, San Diego: UC Medical Center.

Terborg, J. R. (1977), 'Women in management: a research review', *Journal of Applied Psychology,* **62,** 647–64.

Thackray, J. (1979), 'The Feminist Manager', *Management Today,* **152,** Apr., 90–7.

Theorell, T., & Rahe, R. H. (1974),'Psychological Characteristics of subjects with myocardial infarction in Stockholm', in *Life of Stress and Illness,* Gunderson, E., & Rahe, R. H. (eds), Springfield, Illinois: Charles C. Thomas, 90–104.

Toynbee, P. (1981), 'If the radical resolutions put forward were acted on by the European Parliament, feminism would be defunct', *The Guardian,* 6 Feb. 1981.

Training Services Division, MSC (1981), *No Barriers Here? – A Guide to Career Development Issues in the Employment of Women,* Leicester: HMSO.

Waldron, I. (1978), 'Type A behaviour pattern and coronary heart disease in men and women', *Social Science Medicine,* **12B,** 167–170.

Waldron, I., Zyzanski, S., Shekelle, R.B., *et al.* (1977), 'The coronary-prone behaviour pattern in employed men and women', *Journal of Human Stress,* **3,** 2–18.

Wanless, T. (1981), 'Women in management: some managers are more equal than others', *The Business Graduate,* XI, 1, Spring, 14–15.

Weiner, J., Nierenberg, G. & Goldstein, N. (1976), in Larwood, L. & Wood, M. M. (1977), *Women in Management,* London: Lexington Books.

Weiner, A., Marten, S. Wochnick, E., Davis, M., Fishman, R., & Clayton, J. (1979), 'Psychiatric disorders among professional women', *Archives of General Psychiatry,* **36,** 169–73.

Welsh, M. A., (1980), *Networking, The Great New Way for Women to Get Ahead,* United States.

Wilkinson, M. (1980), *Migraine and Other Headaches,* London: Tavistock, BMA.

Wilsnack, S. C. (1973),'Femininity by the bottle', *Psychology Today,* Apr., 39–43.

Wingerson, L. (1981), 'Executive women – healthier than thou?,*New Scientist,* **91,** 17 Sept., 718–21.

Women's Who's Who (1977), London: Women in Management.

Wood, M. M. (1975), 'What does it take for a woman to make it in management?', *Personnel Journal,* **66,** 38–41.

Wood, M. M. (1978), 'Women in management: how is it working out', in Stead, B. A. (ed.), *Women in Management,* Englewood Cliffs, New Jersey: Prentice–Hall Inc.

Woolman, C., & Frank, H. (1975), 'The sole woman in a professional peer group', *American Journal of Orthopsychiatry,* **45,** 164–71.

Index